Terrorists and Terrorist Groups

Other titles in the Lucent Terrorism Library are:

America Under Attack: Primary Sources
America Under Attack: September 11, 2001
The History of Terrorism

Terrorists and Terrorist Groups

Stephen Currie

Natick High School
Library

LUCENT BOOKS
SAN DIEGO, CALIFORNIA

THOMSON
——✳——™
GALE

*Detroit • New York • San Diego • San Francisco
Boston • New Haven, Conn. • Waterville, Maine
London • Munich*

Library of Congress Cataloging-in-Publication Data

Currie, Stephen, 1960–
    Terrorists and terrorist groups / by Stephen Currie.
        p.   cm. — (Terrorism library series)
Summary: Discusses the formation, political agenda, actions, and religious beliefs of various groups
that use violent means to achieve their ends.
Includes bibliographical references and index.
    ISBN 1-59018-207-3 (hardback : alk. paper)
    1. Terrorism—Juvenile literature. 2. Terrorists—Juvenile literature. [1. Terrorism.] I. Title.   II. Series.
    HV6431 .C88 2002
    303.6'25—dc21

2001007843

Contents

Foreword

It was the bloodiest day in American history since the battle of Antietam during the Civil War—a day in which everything about the nation would change forever. People, when speaking of the country, would henceforth specify "before September 11" or "after September 11." It was as if, on that Tuesday morning, the borders had suddenly shifted to include Canada and Mexico, or as if the official language of the United States had changed. The difference between "before" and "after" was that pronounced.

That Tuesday morning, September 11, 2001, was the day that Americans began to learn firsthand about terrorism, as one fuel-heavy commercial airliner, and then another, hit New York's World Trade Towers—sending them thundering to the ground in a firestorm of smoke and ash. A third airliner was flown into a wall of the Pentagon in Washington, D.C., and a fourth was apparently wrestled away from terrorists before it could be steered into another building. By the time the explosions and collapses had stopped and the fires had been extinguished, more than three thousand Americans had died.

Film clips and photographs showed the horror of that day. Trade Center workers could be seen leaping to their deaths from seventy, eighty, ninety floors up rather than endure the 1,000-degree temperatures within the towers. New Yorkers who had thought they were going to work, were caught on film desperately racing the other way to escape the wall of dust and debris that rolled down the streets of lower Manhattan. Photographs showed badly burned Pentagon secretaries and frustrated rescue workers. Later pictures would show huge fire engines buried under the rubble.

It was not the first time America had been the target of terrorists. The same World Trade Center had been targeted in 1993 by Islamic terrorists, but the results had been negligible. The worst of such acts on American soil came in 1995 at the hands of a home-grown terrorist whose hatred for the government led to the bombing of the federal building in Oklahoma City. The blast killed 168 people—19 of them children.

But the September 11 attacks were far different. It was terror on a frighteningly well-planned, larger scale, carried out by nineteen men from the Middle East whose hatred of the United States drove them to the most appalling suicide mission the world had ever witnessed. As one U.S. intelligence officer told a CNN reporter, "These guys turned airplanes into weapons of mass destruction, landmarks familiar to all of us into mass graves."

Some observers say that September 11 may always be remembered as the date that the people of the United States finally came face to face with terrorism. "You've been relatively sheltered from terrorism," says an Israeli terrorism expert. "You hear about it happening here in the Middle East, in Northern Ireland, places far away from you. Now Americans have joined the real world where this ugliness is almost a daily occurrence."

This "real world" presents a formidable challenge to the United States and other nations. It is a world in which there are no rules, where modern terrorism is war not waged on soldiers, but on innocent people – including children. Terrorism is meant to shatter people's hope, to create instability in their daily lives, to make them feel vulnerable and frightened. People who continue to feel unsafe will demand that their leaders make concessions—*do something*—so that terrorists will stop the attacks.

Many experts feel that terrorism against the United States is just beginning. "The tragedy is that other groups, having seen [the success of the September 11 attacks] will think: why not do something else?" says Richard Murphy, former ambassador to Syria and Saudi Arabia. "This is the beginning of their war. There is a mentality at work here that the West is not prepared to understand."

Because terrorism is abhorrent to the vast majority of the nations on the planet, President George W. Bush's declaration of war against terrorism was supported by many other world leaders. He reminded citizens that it would be a long war, and one not easily won. However, as many agree, there is no choice; if terrorism is allowed to continue unchecked the world will never be safe.

The four volumes of the Lucent Terrorism Library help to explain the unexplainable events of September 11, 2001, as well as examine the history and personalities connected with terrorism in the United States and elsewhere in the world. Annotated bibliographies provide readers with ideas for further research. Fully documented primary and secondary source quotations enliven the text. Each book in this series provides students with a wealth of information as well as launching points for further study and discussion.

The Terrorists

The end of the twentieth century has been called the era of terrorism. Indeed, some observers have called the problem of worldwide terror the central issue of the period. During the last part of that century and into the early years of the next, terrorist attacks have taken place across the globe, from the Middle East to South America and from Europe to the United States. The perpetrators have come from all walks of life and have used a variety of deadly and diabolic weapons to carry out their plans. Whatever their origins and their methods, however, the outcomes are the same: the injury and death of innocent people for the cause of a political goal.

The use of violence for political purposes is hardly new. From the beginning of recorded time, people have waged wars against one another in the hopes of gaining territory, increasing wealth, or wielding political power. But the terrorism of the twentieth century is in some significant ways different from standard wars.

One difference is that wars are generally fought between nations, wheras terrorists are usually separate from governments. Another difference involves the importance and meaning of rules. Despite all their brutality, wars keep a veneer of civilization because they tend to follow a set of agreed-upon regulations. Terrorists, on the other hand, scorn traditional rules of warfare when they carry out their attacks. Finally, and perhaps most importantly, armies are supposed to avoid the killing of innocent civilians as much as possible. Terrorists, however, make a point of striking at ordinary, innocent citizens.

Defining a Terrorist

It is difficult to define a terrorist with precision. The U.S. government has offered one frequently cited definition. According to the definition, terrorism means "premeditated, politically motivated violence." To be classified as terrorism, the violence must be aimed at civilians, and perpetrators must be "subnational groups or clandestine agents"[1]—in other words, not an army belonging to any officially recognized state or government.

This definition, however, is controversial. An old saying argues that one man's terrorist is another's freedom fighter, and there is certainly some truth to this notion. People are indeed more tolerant of the slaughter of civilians when they agree with the goals of the killers. To at least some residents of Northern Ireland, for example, members of the Irish Republican Army—terrorists to most of the

A boy leaps over a puddle as a bombed truck smolders in a Catholic neighborhood of East Belfast, Northern Ireland.

rest of the world—are heroes because they fight British oppression. The same is true of some Palestinians and the group Hamas, which engages in violent acts that hurt or kill Israeli citizens.

Ideology and Politics

Terrorists today come in many different forms. A few belong to no organized groups and work largely on their own. Others recruit thousands of supporters and build up extensive networks of terror. Some terrorist organizations lead splashy but brief lives in the news: They figure prominently in national affairs over a period of several years and then disappear. Still others persist through generations.

Terrorist goals also vary considerably. A few terrorist groups, especially those that have been among the longest lasting, say they are working for the capture and control of land on behalf of a people, culture, or religion. Other groups that use terror have goals that have more to do with political systems and government than with land and people. It is their stated purpose to replace what they see as a corrupt or useless system of government with another model or idea. This is what is known as political ideology, which is often expressed in terms of a line or a spectrum. Conservatives are seen as holding a position somewhere on the right of this line; hence the term "right-wing" to describe their views. Liberals are correspondingly referred to as "left-wing." In much of the world, these positions move gradually into each other and coexist peacefully. Terrorists motivated by political philosophy, though, tend toward either a right- or left-wing extreme. The American bomber Timothy McVeigh, for example, held a dramatically right-wing perspective, while the Peruvian group Shining Path had as its goal the establishment of an extreme left-wing state.

But whatever the motivation, what marks terrorism, at heart, is hatred. It takes deep and compelling hatred to kill innocent people. Timothy McVeigh, for instance, chose as his target a building that housed a day care center. He knew children would die in the course of making his political statement, yet he carried out his plan regardless. Hamas leaders carry bombs into crowded Middle Eastern stores in order to murder Israeli citizens. The goal may be winning the land or establishing a new political order, but hatred is what makes it possible to kill innocent people in order to achieve that goal.

Indeed, there may be no better example of terrorist hatred than that expressed in late 2001 by Osama bin Laden, the leader of the international terrorist organization al-Qaeda. Bin Laden's anger at the United States and its Western allies was so great that he ordered his followers to destroy several thousand American lives. The action was carried out even though bin Laden could not expect to win new territory or cultural benefit, although there was no discernible political philosophy behind the attack. As bin Laden's case demonstrates, the roots of terrorist activity lie mainly in hatred.

Chapter One

Hamas

The Middle East has been called the birthplace of modern terrorism. Sparked by centuries-old conflicts between members of various religions, and made worse by more recent political disputes, the region produced one violent group after another during the twentieth century. The violence has not been spread evenly across the area, however. By far the greatest proportion of Middle Eastern terror centers on a conflict in a small part of the region—a land known to Arabs as Palestine and to Jews as Israel.

Although the last fifty years have been particularly troublesome in Israel, the issues there have their roots in ancient history. For political, historical, and religious reasons, Muslims, Jews, and Christians have each claimed parts or all of the land, and they usually have not been willing or able to discuss their differences in peaceful ways. The result has been continued tensions in the area, tensions so great that they have given rise to a number of terrorist groups.

Of all these groups, perhaps the most powerful—and the most complicated—is the Islamic resistance organization known as Hamas. Hamas was originally formed to protect and support Arab Palestinians—nearly all of them Muslim—against the perceived evils of the more powerful Jewish Israeli government. In recent years, the group's leaders have undertaken many attacks against Israeli citizens with the goal of eliminating Israeli control of certain parts of the region—and perhaps overthrowing Israel as a nation altogether. Among terrorist groups today, Hamas is noted for the violence and destruction of its attacks, for its unwillingness to compromise, and for the depth of its popular support in its own home base.

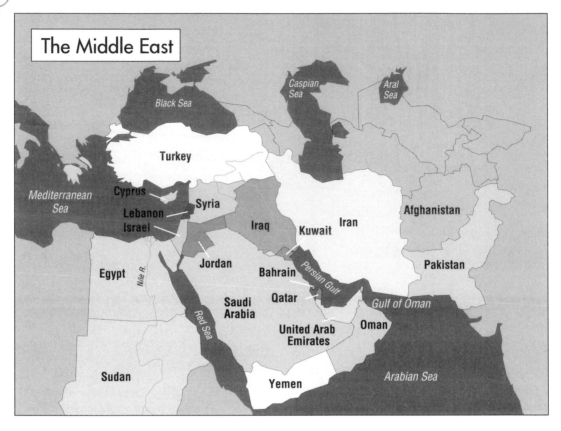

The Middle East

Caspian Sea

Aral Sea

Black Sea

Turkey

Mediterranean Sea

Cyprus

Syria

Lebanon

Israel

Iraq

Kuwait

Iran

Afghanistan

Egypt

Nile R.

Jordan

Bahrain

Persian Gulf

Pakistan

Qatar

Saudi Arabia

United Arab Emirates

Gulf of Oman

Oman

Red Sea

Sudan

Yemen

Arabian Sea

Israel and the Palestinians

Hamas can be seen as one response to the complex set of problems stemming from the complicated history of Israel and Palestine. In ancient times, Israel had been the center of Jewish existence. In fact, the area held a special place in Jewish history: According to the Old Testament, it was the land that God had given to Abraham and his descendants. Since Jews consider Abraham a founder of their faith, many Jews believe that the land encompassed by the biblical Israel is by rights under the control of Judaism and therefore of the Jewish people.

But the influence of Jews in Israel did not last much past the days of the Old Testament, especially after Islam was founded during the seventh century A.D. Islam quickly gained the allegiance of the majority of the people in and around the biblical Israel. Over time, the remaining Jews began to leave the region. By the nineteenth century, very few Jews lived in the area. Those who remained complained bitterly of mistreatment at the hands of their Muslim rulers and their Arab neighbors, most of them Muslim as well. But the greatest number of Palestinian Jews had moved from Israel altogether. They had scattered into Europe and elsewhere in search of better lives.

Nevertheless, Jews did not lose sight of the claim they had made to Israel. Late in the nineteenth century, several Jewish thinkers came up with a doctrine they called Zionism, which called for the reestablishment of a Jewish homeland in Palestine. At first, Zionism was mostly an abstract notion. During World War II, however, the Nazi Holocaust killed an estimated 6 million people, most of them Jewish, and the search for a Jewish state suddenly became of the essence. In 1948, the United Nations helped carve out Israel as a separate nation and a safe haven for Jews, to be governed according to Jewish principles.

Much of the area's Arab population was furious. The region chosen to become the new country was home to many Muslims who called themselves Palestinians. Although they shared a religion with nearby nations, they saw themselves as a separate people; they did not feel a part of Jordan, Syria, Lebanon, or other Middle Eastern countries. The Israeli government allowed Muslims to continue living in Israel and permitted them to take part in most areas of national life. Still, many Palestinians fled the country, and those who remained were far from comfortable with the new government.

Israel's new neighbors were not any happier with the situation. The Arab nations surrounding Israel did not support a Jewish state and took the Palestinians' side in the dispute. Some questioned Israel's right to exist and the United Nations' role in establishing a Jewish homeland. The result, soon enough, was violence. During the 1960s and '70s, both Syria and Egypt fought wars against Israel.

Hostility and the Intifada

The wars, however, settled little. With greater firepower and better military organization, Israel not only repelled invasion but also took

the opportunity to expand into former Arab territory. In particular, Israel took over three important sections just outside its allotted borders: the West Bank, Golan Heights, and the Gaza Strip. All three regions had heavy Palestinian populations—far too many people to easily absorb into Israel or to force out in favor of Jewish settlers, although some Jews did begin to move into the areas in question. More than ever, Arab nationalists—those who opposed Israel and wanted a separate Islamic Palestinian state—bitterly resented the situation.

Several groups formed during these years to work for Palestinian rights. Among the best known of these was the Palestinian Liberation Organization (PLO), run by Palestinian leader Yasir Arafat. Another group

Yasir Arafat is the leader of the Palestinian Liberation Organization, one of several groups that works for Palestinian rights.

was a Gaza Strip organization known as the Muslim Brotherhood. Initially, the Muslim Brotherhood functioned as a social service organization for Palestinian Arabs. Patterned after similar organizations in other Arab countries, the Gaza branch had been founded by Ahmed Yassin, a Palestinian born in 1938.

Yassin had been confined to a wheelchair since a diving accident during his teenage years, nevertheless he was a strong voice in the Palestinian community. Several other Palestinian organizations—including Arafat's PLO—instigated violent attacks on Israeli police and civilians. On Yassin's instructions, however, members of the Muslim Brotherhood avoided violence. They chose instead to work for the advancement of Palestinians through education and increased business opportunities.

But by the 1980s, Gaza's Muslim Brotherhood was losing its influence. Its quiet, peaceful ways were being overshadowed by the angrier rhetoric of more violent groups. Palestinians increasingly favored more assertive action against the Israeli government. When several members of the PLO accused the Muslim Brotherhood of being pawns of Israel, Yassin decided it was time to become a more active opponent of Israel and its occupation of Gaza. By 1984, he was urging his followers to resist Israel: through peaceful civil disobedience if possible, but by using armed attacks if necessary.

The Palestinian situation worsened throughout the 1980s. Tensions rose higher and higher with every grenade, every shooting, every new settler. In 1987, Palestinians on the Gaza Strip and in the West Bank staged a long-term mass uprising that became known as the Intifada, from an Arabic word meaning "to shake." Over the next six years, angry Palestinians staged strikes, attacked armed Israeli soldiers, and vandalized government property. Israeli officials responded harshly, using riot gear to disperse crowds and hauling many of the protesters away to prison.

The Intifada further changed Yassin's perspective. After watching Israeli responses to the protests, Yassin no longer believed that any peaceful tactics could be effective. Instead, he embraced violence as the only possible

Ahmed Yassin is the founder of Hamas, an Islamic militant group that has used violence to protest the existence of Israel.

solution to the Israeli control of Gaza. Although he did not entirely disband the Muslim Brotherhood, he and several other Palestinians set up a new and separate organization, which they called the Islamic Resistance Movement. The group was usually referred to, however, by its Arabic acronym, Hamas—a word that translates to "zeal."

Ideology and Religion

The name was appropriate. Hamas sprang directly from a zealous Muslim fundamentalism, a very rigid and intolerant adherence to a particular idea or belief. Hamas's fundamentalism was based on the group's own interpretation of Islamic principles. Many Muslims condemned Hamas's interpretation both then and now, charging that the group distorted genuine Islamic thought. Nevertheless, the organization saw itself as following the will of Allah, the Arabic word for God, and Yassin and other leaders of the group referred frequently to the Koran—the holiest book of Islam—to determine strategy and justify their actions.

The belief that Hamas was divinely inspired helped give group members confidence that their actions were right. It also led to a demonization of Palestine's enemies. Allah was with the rebels, Hamas leaders argued, while the Israelis were on the devil's side. Hamas immediately began to attract preachers and professors who appreciated the organization's apparent devotion to conservative Islamic ideas. Many of these new members were noticeably more militant than Yassin and some of the other founders of the group. Indeed, the new members included some of the most radical Arabs anywhere in Palestine.

In 1988, Hamas formally called for the launching of a holy war, or jihad, against Israel. The group demanded "the liberation of Palestine in its entirety, from the [Mediterranean] Sea to the [Jordan] River"[2] a region encompassing not only the disputed Gaza Strip and West Bank, but all of present-day Israel as well. In late 1988, Hamas started distributing leaflets throughout the Gaza Strip urging violent resistance to Israeli rule. "Spare no efforts [to fan] the fire of the uprising,"[3] commanded one typical example.

The Israeli government reacted swiftly. That October, police arrested several dozen Hamas supporters on suspicion of inciting rebellion. But the arrests only strengthened Hamas's resolve. Group members argued that the arrests were not truly motivated by the threat of violence against Israel but, rather, by the conservative theology espoused by Hamas. Fearing that Israel's real target was Islam itself, more Palestinians began to join the new movement.

More Arrests

Over the next few months, Hamas carried out a number of violent attacks on Israeli civilians, and more and more members of the movement were arrested. By the spring of 1989, about 250 Hamas supporters were in prison. However, Hamas was still seen more as an annoyance than as a real threat to Israeli security. That perception changed permanently in May 1989, when two Israeli soldiers were murdered while hitchhiking near the Gaza Strip.

In response to the murders, Israeli officials immediately rounded up a number of Hamas activists, including Yassin, and charged them with causing the deaths of the two soldiers. That September, with Yassin and others still in custody, Israel took the unusual step of banning the organization altogether. Anyone who joined or remained a member risked imprisonment. Hamas was the first Palestinian resistance group to be officially outlawed; it would not be the last.

At his trial, Yassin denied the specific charges of planning the murders but was happy to take responsibility for helping to found, organize, and fund Hamas. As his lawyer reported, "My client says it is not just his right but his obligation to establish this organization to battle the [Israeli] occupation. He is not sorry for what he did."[4] Yassin's denials of direct wrongdoing, however, were to no avail. The Israeli court sentenced him to life in prison.

Despite—or perhaps because of—the Israeli ban, Hamas continued to grow in size and importance. One arm of the organization resumed some of its earlier community-building and charitable activities, while another arm dedicated itself to religious education. The best-known group of Hamas members, however, formed the al-Qassam Brigades, a paramilitary organization (that is, an unofficial army) dedicated to committing acts of terror against Israelis, especially in and around the Gaza Strip.

In 1993, Arafat and the PLO signed a peace agreement with Yitzhak Rabin, then prime minister of Israel. Among other things, the agreement called for the establishment of a PLO-dominated Palestinian Authority to rule Gaza in conjunction with the Israeli government. The agreement, reached after many weeks of negotiations, was a major success for moderates on both sides. Weary of war, many Israelis found themselves increasingly willing to accept some kind of a Palestinian state in exchange for peace, and many Palestinians were likewise ready to put the battles behind them.

However, the peace deal did not suit extreme sentiments on either side. Radical Zionists saw the agreement as nothing more than giving away vital parts of Israeli territory to the enemy. Similarly, Hamas and other radical Islamic groups scorned Arafat's willingness to negotiate with Israel at all. In their view, such negotiations were equivalent to stating that Israel had the right to exist.

Within the next year, Hamas began the task of derailing the peace agreement. In October 1994, the organization carried out three major attacks against Israeli civilians. First, Hamas gunmen fired randomly into an Israeli café district, leaving two dead. Then they kidnapped and murdered an Israeli soldier. Finally, a terrorist blew up a bus in Tel Aviv, killing more than twenty Israelis and wounding another forty. Hamas had put Israel and the Palestinian Authority on notice: To members of this Palestinian group, at least, the peace talks were completely unacceptable.

Against Israel—and Arafat

These terrorist activities were primarily attacks on Israel, of course. The people killed in the violence were Israelis; the property

Israeli prime minister Yitzhak Rabin (left) and Yasir Arafat (right) shake hands as President Bill Clinton presides at the 1993 peace meeting between Israel and the Palestinians.

destroyed was Israeli as well. Deeply shaken by the violence, Israeli officials spoke out angrily against the terrorists. "No enemy will defeat us," promised Prime Minister Rabin, who had signed the peace accord on behalf of his country. "We will fight Hamas until we have destroyed it."[5]

Indeed, Israelis had good reason to feel such fury. After years of fighting, peace had at last seemed a genuine possibility. National leaders had made what they believed were significant compromises in order to reach a deal. But the peace talks had not, in fact, stopped the terror. If anything, the situation

had grown worse. It was abundantly clear that some Palestinians were unalterably opposed to a peace deal of any kind.

In a deeper sense, the Hamas attacks were aimed not just at Israel but at Arafat, the PLO, and the peace process itself. Through its violence, Hamas hoped to destroy any chance of arriving at peace terms that might appeal to Israeli leaders. In the eyes of Hamas officials, Arafat and his organization had sold out the interests of ordinary Palestinians. Since Hamas objected to the concessions Arafat was offering, the violence was at least partly intended to express dissatisfaction with

Arafat's decision—and to call into question his authority to make such decisions in the first place.

In this goal, Hamas was largely successful. The Hamas bombings put Arafat in a difficult position. According to the terms of the peace treaty, Arafat and his Palestinian Authority were responsible for helping to suppress terrorism in Gaza and the West Bank. By going after Hamas, he would offend conservatives; he would be seen as Israel's puppet, ignoring the needs of the Palestinian people in his hurry to do Israel's bidding. But if he did not take a hard line with the terrorists, he risked jeopardizing the peace agreement.

Arafat chose to work for peace. Over the next few days, Palestinian police arrested four hundred suspected Hamas sympathizers. The action angered thousands of religious conservatives who believed that the attack on Israel was justified. Many Palestinians rallied outside the jails in support of those imprisoned. "It was worse than during the intifada," said one disaffected Palestinian, "because [this time] Palestinians were thrown in prison by people they loved, the Palestinian police."[6]

Still, Arafat's actions did not stop the violence. Over the next few years, those members of Hamas who remained free continued to plan and stage attacks against Israeli citizens. The intensity of the terror came and went, but the threat was always there, and it was rare for more than a month or so to pass without at least one violent outburst from Hamas. As long as peace was a possibility under terms other than those favored by the terrorists, Hamas operatives were not ready to give up their struggle.

Suicide Bombers

The series of Hamas attacks that began in 1994 tended to be more bloody and violent than those of earlier years. In part, this was due to Hamas's increased experience in terrorism. In part, too, it was because of the reality of the peace agreement, which served to focus the discontent of many Palestinians. But the years also marked a significant shift in Hamas's strategies and tactics.

During its history, Hamas had made use of many weapons and strategies, employing everything from guns to stones to small homemade bombs in carrying out its terrorist goals. But in the mid-1990s, the group began to make extensive use of an especially chilling weapon: the suicide bomber. Suicide bombers, for the most part, are young, unmarried men willing to sacrifice themselves for their cause. These terrorists deliberately destroy their own lives in the process of blowing up innocent civilians. Because they have no intention of trying to escape, they can get close to a crowd and create a great deal of damage.

The list of suicide bombings by Hamas is long. In early 1996, for example, about sixty people were killed in suicide attacks over a period of less than two weeks. In September 1997, three bombers attacked a bustling pedestrian district in downtown Jerusalem. In August 2001, another Hamas bomber detonated an explosive in a Jerusalem pizza parlor, killing fifteen and wounding many more. Later that same year, twenty-one died in an attack on Tel Aviv.

Hamas is not the first group to use suicide as a weapon of terror. Some Japanese pilots flew airplanes into military targets during World War II, and several other Middle Eastern guerrilla groups made use of suicide bombers before Hamas was even founded. But Hamas has used suicide bombers so often and so effectively that the technique has become closely identified with the group. In all, Hamas suicide bombers have killed perhaps three hundred people.

The operations carried out by suicide bombers are not complicated. Sometimes a suicide bomber will simply drive a booby-trapped car into a crowded city street. When the driver steers the car into a store window or a lamppost, the vehicle explodes, killing the bomber and many bystanders as well. Sometimes a volunteer straps dynamite to his belt and walks into a public place. At the right moment, he detonates the device by means of a small switch kept in his pants pocket. The result is the same.

Hamas leaders have no trouble finding men who are willing to carry out these missions. For the most part, Hamas leaders recruit bombers from the ranks of the poor and unemployed. Those who accept the assignment are promised that their families will receive money in appreciation for their work and sacrifice. They are also told that they will be honored by their survivors. "It's like a wedding day for him," says Yassin about the funeral of a suicide bomber. "His death is like a celebration—we offer candy, sweets and cold drinks, because we know he'll be so high in heaven."[7]

Hamas's interpretation of Islam promises immediate glory in the afterlife to those who die defending their faith. According to Hamas, those who die in suicide attacks go directly to paradise. But, in fact, many would-be bombers seem to need very little encouragement from

Two Israeli border police officers walk away from a bus that was destroyed by a suicide bomber in Jerusalem.

religious doctrine to take part in the attacks. Israeli control of Palestine is itself enough to spark some men to volunteer. Angry and frustrated at Israel's presence and policies, some of the suicide bombers are prepared to do whatever they can to stop their enemies.

Cycle of Violence

Since the events of 1994, not much has changed in this part of the Middle East. On most issues, Israel and Palestine remain very far apart. The two sides have not been able to work out the details of a lasting peace, perhaps in part because Hamas has continued to stage attacks aimed at sabotaging the peace process. Hamas's terrorist violence, mostly bombs and shootings in the heart of Israel, has usually served to upset the rather fragile understanding that exists between the two peoples. It certainly does not help bring the two sides any closer together.

Not only do Hamas attacks injure and kill innocent Israeli citizens, but they give rise to anger among those who are not directly affected by the terror. Even though the Hamas terrorists make up only a small part of the Palestinian population, to many Israelis, they seem representative of all Palestine—and all Islam as well. "They just want to kill," says a conservative Israeli mayor about Muslims in general. "It's not an eye for an eye. It's an eye, and another eye, and another eye and another eye. . . ."[8] Such stereotypes help silence the voice of moderation in the Middle East.

In turn, Hamas terrorism has led to angry responses on the part of Israel and its citizens. Some of these responses have been terrorist actions by any definition. In early 1994, for instance, a radical Israeli, Baruch Goldstein, set off a bomb that killed thirty Palestinians. Goldstein was quickly arrested by Israeli police, and Israeli officials cracked down on militant Zionists within the country in an effort to keep the peace process alive.

However, violence has also been aimed at Palestine by Israeli officials themselves. Israeli police frequently use violence to put down Palestinian demonstrations, for example; in some cases, soldiers have shot and killed protesters armed only with stones. They have also sent agents to assassinate Hamas leaders, along with members of other Palestinian terrorist groups. In November 2001, for instance, Israeli helicopters shot antitank missiles at a car in which senior Hamas official Mahmoud Abu Hanoud was riding. Abu Hanoud was killed instantly.

These acts are intended to control the violence, but more often they seem to inflame it. That is especially true when Israeli responses endanger civilians as well as terrorist leaders. In one July 2001 attack, for instance, missiles aimed at Hamas headquarters killed two members of the group's leadership—and two small children waiting for their non-Hamas parents on the street below. The following November, Israeli officials hid bombs in a residential section of Gaza thought to be frequented by Hamas leaders. The bombs were accidentally set off instead by five Palestinian schoolchildren, all of whom died.

Just as Hamas terrorism alienates moderate Jews, Israeli responses such as these alienate the moderate Palestinians who represent the strongest hope for a lasting peace.

At best, they confirm for many Arabs the notion that Israel is not to be trusted. At worst, they drive these moderates into having sympathy for the terrorists. This is even true for those who are not attracted by Hamas's conservative brand of Islam. "I'm not religious," said one Palestinian man shortly after the July 2001 attack, "but if Hamas fights the occupation I have all the respect for Hamas."[9]

The constant terrorism has also put a great deal of pressure on Yasir Arafat. At times he has responded to Hamas violence very much as he did in 1993—by arresting as many suspected Hamas members as the Palestinian police force can find. In 1996, for instance, following a wave of bombings, he arrested dozens of terrorist sympathizers and other militants. He also shut down a number of Palestinian social service organizations at that time, arguing that they were only fronts for the terrorists. In 1998, following another attack aimed at Israeli children, Arafat did the same.

Israeli police clash with an Arab Israeli who was protesting the construction of a highway on Arab land.

Palestinian women shout in protest of Israel's use of force to stop the Palestinian uprising.

At other times, though, Arafat has been less willing to arrest the terrorists. In the fall of 2000, another wave of Palestinian protests against Israel began, and the popularity of Hamas and similar organizations climbed dramatically. Since then, despite intense pressure from Israel and many other nations, Arafat has not cracked down against the terrorists. Some see this decision as an indication of Hamas's growing support; in this view, Arafat now must fear the terrorists more than he fears Israel. Others, less sympathetic, charge that Arafat's choice reflects his pol-

itics, and indicates that he has adopted Hamas's goals and attitudes.

Political Theory and Discussions

To an extent, Hamas has been involved in political discussions rather than simply spreading terror. There is a political arm of the organization that investigates possible solutions to Middle Eastern violence, and members of the PLO have at times considered inviting Hamas to form a political party and help run the Palestinian Authority.

Indeed, several Hamas officials have occasionally expressed some willingness to bargain directly with the Israelis themselves.

That has been perhaps particularly true of the organization's founder, Ahmed Yassin. Released from jail by Israel as part of a prisoner swap in 1997, Yassin today plays a small day-to-day role in the running of the organization. He is now almost blind and nearly deaf, in addition to remaining wheelchair-bound; he has difficulty breathing and has trouble making himself understood while he speaks. Nevertheless, he is widely respected in Palestine, and he serves as Hamas's spiritual leader.

Yassin's return to Palestine after his release from prison was marked by angry words and hard feelings. In his view, things had failed to improve since the signing of the peace agreement between Israel and the PLO. "Israeli soldiers [still] control the roads and borders and prevent our freedom of movement," he told a reporter. "True, they do not come into my house anymore, but the Israelis are still here, working through their collaborators." [10] Who he meant by the "collaborators" was clear to all his listeners: Arafat and the Palestinian Authority.

However, Yassin surprised many observers by offering a plan for Middle Eastern peace upon his release. To be sure, the plan was extremely one-sided; Yassin's demands included the establishment of a totally independent Palestinian state and the immediate withdrawal of Israel from all its territories acquired since its founding. Israeli officials were at first pleased that Yassin showed signs of a willingness to negotiate, even though they were not

at all inclined to accept his proposal as it stood. But whether because Yassin was insincere in his offer or because other leaders of the group quickly overruled him, nothing came of the suggestion.

Hamas Today

Today, Hamas continues to tread a fine line between fighting a war of religion and a war of politics and territory. The fundamentalist beginnings of the organization argue strongly for the first, and much of the group's rhetoric and strategies reflect that leaning. In this view, the conflict is a sacred conflict between members of two very different religious groups, with God on the side of the Islamic terrorists. "Allah akbar [God is great]," reads the concluding line of several Hamas leaflets. "Death to the occupiers." [11]

Yet, at the same time, some members of Hamas have been careful not to cast the struggle entirely in religious terms. "We are not fighting the Jews because they are Jews," Yassin said shortly after his release from prison. "We are fighting to remove the occupation over us and our people. We, the Palestinian people, are the victims of an Israeli aggression . . . on our homeland." [12] In this view, the problem is not religious as much as territorial.

Regardless of the reasons, Hamas has always been insistent that the Palestinians have the right to use terror against Israelis, even civilians, since the Palestinians have been themselves the victims of violent aggression. As Yassin put it in early 1998, Palestinians have little choice in the matter. "If you are on the road and somebody shoots at you, do you

Hamas activists burn an Israeli flag in celebration of Ahmed Yassin's release from prison in 1997.

take your gun and shoot back?" he asked rhetorically. "Do you protect yourself or do you keep silent?"[13]

Casting Palestinians as the victims has been an important part of Hamas's ideology—and an equally important part of the group's appeal. According to orthodox Islamic ideas, there is no justification for murdering innocent civilians. Hamas, however, has argued with some success that its own violence is justified by Israel's actions. According to this view, Israeli activity in Palestine has turned ordinary citizens into combatants. "Islam says don't kill children," admits one terrorist. "But during a war, children are killed, and we are in a war. If children get killed, it is God's will."[14] This Hamas perspective has been accepted by many Palestinians who might otherwise disapprove of the organization because of its terrorist tactics.

Hamas continues to fight toward its goal of establishing Islamic control throughout

Palestine—and most likely, all of Israel as well. The group has shown itself to be bitterly opposed to any peace proposal that would compromise its ideals, and it has demonstrated time and again that it is willing to defend its position through violence. Moreover, Hamas continues to earn the support of a substantial minority of Palestinians. Because of the group's methods and uncompromising ideology, Hamas remains one of the most dangerous and influential forces in the world today.

Chapter Two

Abimael Guzman and Shining Path

Of all terrorist organizations past and present, Peru's Shining Path has been perhaps the most uncompromisingly brutal. For about a dozen years, Shining Path—"Sendero Luminosa" in Spanish—carried out regular terrorist operations in Peru. The organization mixed revolutionary rhetoric with an astonishing level of violence. Between 1980 and 1992, its activities threw Peru into domestic turmoil, depopulated hundreds of villages, and left about twenty-seven thousand people dead.

The story of Shining Path is tightly connected to the story of its leader, Abimael Guzman. A college professor with an interest in political philosophy, Guzman was the group's founder and chief strategist. For twelve years, Guzman evaded capture by Peruvian authorities, all the while using his charismatic personality and his political appeals to attract new members to Shining Path's cause. In a very real way, Guzman *was* Shining Path—a fact that became abundantly clear when Guzman was at last captured and imprisoned in 1992.

Early Years

Abimael Guzman was born on December 3, 1934, near the Peruvian seaport of Mollendo. In his earliest years, young Abimael lived in a two-room house with his mother. His father, a well-off merchant and importer from Peru's upper middle class, lived in somewhat more comfortable circumstances down the street; Guzman's father and mother never married each other. When Abimael was five, his mother died, and he moved in with an uncle. A few years later, he joined his father, stepmother, and several half-brothers. The family soon moved to Arequipa in the southern part of Peru.

In Arequipa, Guzman attended a private high school run by the Catholic Church. He did extremely well; he not only graduated near the top of his class but also won an award for good conduct. In 1953, Guzman went on to an Arequipa college, where he studied philosophy, logic, and law, and became enthralled in his work. Guzman took several classes with a professor named Miguel Angel Rodriguez Rivas. Rivas was a demanding and dramatic instructor, and he took an immediate liking to Guzman.

Peru, South America

Abimael Guzman, founder of Peru's Shining Path.

were pointless since they did not lift the downtrodden out of poverty. Guzman also argued that oppressed societies had both the right and the responsibility to stage violent revolution.

Influences and Ideals

These were potentially explosive words for Peru, a country run at the time by a military dictatorship. The leaders of the nation were deeply, politically conservative. Their right-wing positions put them in direct opposition to Guzman's Marxist perspectives on many issues. The government was also not especially tolerant of people who held different political opinions. Thus, there was an element of danger in Guzman's enthusiasm for Marxism.

However, Peru's leaders took little notice of Guzman's philosophy. At the time, no one had any notion that Guzman would ever act on his radical ideas. Marxists were not unusual in Peru's academic culture during the 1950s, and nearly all Marxist professors kept their interest in radicalism purely theoretical. Despite their rhetoric, they showed no sign of wanting to lead a violent revolution. There was no reason to suspect that Guzman would be any different.

Indeed, Guzman seemed an especially unlikely candidate to take up violence against the government. A man of refined tastes, he was noted for a love of classical music and great literature. It was hard to imagine him giving up those comforts to wage a bloody rebellion. Moreover, Guzman had grown up in a household of privilege. He had little first-hand knowledge of poverty. His interest in

Through Rivas, Guzman began to study the writings of Karl Marx, a German political philosopher of the nineteenth century. Marx's writings formed the foundation for the economic and political systems of socialism and communism, systems well to the left along the political spectrum. Most notably, Marx advocated the sharing of wealth within and between nations. He also urged the abolition of social and economic classes.

Guzman became deeply intrigued by Marxism, and before long, he joined Peru's Communist Party. He wrote two extensive theses for graduate degrees, both of which strongly reflected Marxist theory. In these theses, he described his belief that elections communism thus appeared to be more an intellectual exercise than a philosophy sparked by a deeply rooted desire to change and better the world.

Guzman also did not appear to be the sort to offend others. He was respected even by those who did not entirely share his political ideas. "Abimael was an outstanding man and always well informed," [15] remembered Rivas, whose political ideas were not nearly as far left as his student's. It was hard for most of his friends to imagine this polite, well-liked professor actually taking up arms against the Peruvian government.

But in 1960, just before he earned his graduate degree, Guzman had an experience that would change him forever. When an earthquake struck Arequipa, several members of the university community were asked to help count the survivors. Guzman was among them. The work took him away from middle-class intellectual life and into the poorest areas of the city. For perhaps the first time, Guzman saw Peru's poor and oppressed not as vague ideas in a dusty textbook but as actual people who needed help.

Ideology

Guzman soon moved to the mountain town of Ayacucho to take a job at a university. There, he became a popular lecturer well known for his courses in Marxism

and revolutionary thought. He soon attracted a following among like-minded left-leaning students, who took every available class with him and listened eagerly to his political discourse. "He was like a priest who gives a very convincing talk, a nice sermon, to his faithful," [16] said a colleague.

At the same time, Guzman began to take a deeper interest in the affairs of nations

The philosophies of Karl Marx (pictured) intrigued Guzman and influenced his political activities.

beyond Peru. He had been an ardent supporter of Fidel Castro, a Communist who seized power in Cuba in 1959. However, in 1964 Guzman decided that the Cuban Revolution was not revolutionary enough. He feared that Castro, once in power, had started to turn his back on true Communist ideology. Guzman charged that Castro was influenced by middle-class values and was not working to benefit the poor.

Looking for a more ideologically pure form of communism, Guzman soon became a follower of the brand practiced by Chinese leader Mao Tse-tung. Several years earlier, Mao had successfully ousted the previous Chinese government through heavy use of guerrilla armies—small groups of fighters who staged surprise attacks against soldiers and civilians. Once in power, Mao had instituted economic, cultural, and educational

Fidel Castro fervently delivers a speech a few days after assuming power in Cuba in 1959.

reforms, which Guzman admired. But perhaps most important for Guzman was Mao's use of violence to carry out his plans.

Mao had indeed made extensive use of violence to achieve power. He had inspired thousands of guerrillas to fight to the death for him and for his ideals. His organization had been brutal in dealing with its enemies, too. In an effort to gain control of territory, Maoist guerrillas had terrorized and murdered many innocent civilians. In addition, not long after Mao had seized power, he embarked on a so-called cultural revolution in which educated city dwellers were forced into the countryside and put to work on farms. Guzman noted how Mao used terror as a means of gaining and keeping control of the country. Twice in the early 1960s, Guzman visited China to learn more about Mao's ideals and activities.

Mao Tse-tung's use of violence to expel the previous Chinese government greatly inspired Guzman.

"The Struggle Will Be Between Two Classes"

Beginning in 1965, Guzman's political leanings became more and more radical. He joined several revolutionary organizations, heaping scorn on the Peruvian government and the social and political elites who supported it—and benefited from it as well. In 1969, breaking with other Peruvian Communists, he founded his own political party: the Communist Party of Peru in the Shining Path of Mariategui. It was named after Jose Carlos

Mariategui, who had created the Peruvian Socialist Party in 1930. The organization was often known simply as Shining Path.

In some ways, Shining Path's ideology was strongly positive. It recommended peace and hoped to banish all evil. The goal of the organization, Guzman wrote, was "a single, irreplaceable new society, without exploited or exploiters, without oppressed or oppressors, without classes, without state, without parties, without democracy, without arms, without wars."[17] But that was in the long run.

31

Before this idealistic vision could be achieved, Peru's government would have to be destroyed. In Guzman's view, government leaders were oppressors and exploiters who used social classes and political parties to divide the public. Those who supported the government would have to be eliminated, too. Guzman accepted the fact that they would not relinquish power easily or peacefully. In the short term, a friend summed up Guzman's philosophy as follows: "The struggle will be between two classes, and one of them will have to die."[18]

Guzman had big plans for his new organization. Slowly and patiently, he began the process of making Shining Path a powerful force within Peru. Over the next eleven years, he built up his organization one careful piece at a time, always staying well within the law of the land. Although he had definite plans for violent revolution, he was insistent that the group carry out no terrorist actions until it was ready to do so. If his followers were not thoroughly committed to their cause, Guzman believed, revolt could never succeed. He knew it would take years to build up that kind of commitment and loyalty.

Guzman's initial followers were drawn from his most enthusiastic students from the university, including Augusta La Torre, a former student whom he married in 1964. He also invited other Peruvian radicals into his organization. However, Guzman was careful to keep out Communists who did not fully agree with his political ideas. Guzman worked to earn power within the university, too, eventually gaining control of faculty appointments. He used this new authority to fill the teaching staff with people who agreed with his political beliefs.

Guzman also hoped to draw support from some of Peru's poorest people. To this end, he went out into the countryside and talked with the Indian farmers who made up the bulk of the region's population. The Indians of Peru had legitimate and long-standing grievances about their treatment. Peru's government and economy had been dominated for years by people of European descent, leaving the farmers poor, landless, and without much representation. Some of the farmers had already staged brief revolts, but these had been brutally put down by the military government. Guzman's words and ideology thus struck a nerve among many of his listeners, and some Indians joined his movement as well. Positions of authority within the organization, however, were rarely filled by the poor.

Final Preparations

In the 1970s, Guzman left Ayacucho for a university in Lima, the capital. There, he continued to recruit followers from among the academic community as well as from among the urban poor. These new followers, in turn, fanned out across Peru to spread the message of revolution. Guzman established informal "people's schools" to teach his ideology to farmers and the urban poor. He sent his disciples into the forests for shooting practice and gave clandestine workshops in the use of explosives.

By the mid-1970s, there were several thousand members of Shining Path, all of them committed Communists and rabidly pro-Guzman. Many had left jobs, friends, and families in their zeal to serve. Guzman maintained tight control over the organization, expelling those who challenged his authority or who disagreed with him on even minor ideological points. He kept up his passion for secrecy, and by all accounts did so with remarkable success. Little by little, he put the machinery in place for violent action against the Peruvian government.

By 1980, Guzman was ready to embark on his campaign of terror. That March, his group formally voted to turn to violence; the few dissenters were kicked out of the organization. A month later, Guzman rallied his troops with a dramatic speech in which he promised violent conflict and a positive result:

The invincible flames of the revolution will grow, turning into lead, into steel, and from the roar of the battle with its unquenchable fire, light will emerge, from the blackness, brightness, and there will be a new world. . . . The reactionary forces [that is, Shining Path's opponents] have dreams of blood . . . their hearts plot evil butchery; they arm themselves to the teeth but they will not triumph. [19]

The Terror Begins

Shining Path's first terrorist act took place on May 18, 1980, the date of Peru's first open elections in years. A number of armed guerrilla fighters stormed a polling place in

A group of women walks through a rural section of Peru. Guzman recruited many farmers and urban poor into Shining Path.

Ayacucho and burned the ballot boxes. In one sense, the action was peculiar. Peru was full of protest groups that had lobbied for free elections. Now, their work had paid off. The political process was becoming more open, and the May election was an indicator of the change.

But Shining Path was not like these other protest groups. As he had explained in his graduate thesis, Guzman was opposed to free elections. He believed that popular elections were ineffective in bringing about real change. They had not eliminated class distinctions and inequality of wealth in democratic countries such as the United States. Moreover, the leaders Guzman most admired were strongly opposed to elections them-

selves. Mao, for example, had never held one. Neither had another hero of Guzman's, the onetime Soviet leader Lenin. Like other Communist rulers, these men believed instead in a long-term class struggle in which the wealthy should have no voice—a goal that did not mesh well with free and fair elections.

Besides, Guzman's overall strategy required widespread discontent among Peruvians. Free elections tended to bring the government closer to the people, and Guzman was anxious to avoid that at all costs. His message of mass rebellion would be most effective, he knew, if the government cracked down harshly on dissenters. The more distant, corrupt, and brutal Peru's leaders became, the more Guzman's

Shining Path guerrilla fighters show off their weapons in Ayacucho, Peru.

message would resonate among the down-trodden of Peru.

The raid on the Ayacucho polling place was only the beginning. By 1982, Shining Path had claimed responsibility for more than five thousand separate acts of terror. By 1986, the figure had risen to twenty-eight thousand. At first, Shining Path had seemed a relatively minor threat compared to several other protest groups within Peru. Before long, though, it had become evident that Shining Path was far more lethal than any other Peruvian organization had ever dreamed of being.

The Attacks

Shining Path's acts of terror could be divided into three rough categories. Much of the violence was intended to disrupt the system of transportation and communication that linked Peru together. Shining Path guerrillas dynamited bridges and blew up railroad tracks. They destroyed telephone wires and television antennas. They shot trucks as they traveled along the country's roadways. In some places, notably Ayacucho, they brought commerce, travel, and communication nearly to a halt. Elsewhere, the occasional damaged road or blasted newspaper office served as a constant reminder of Shining Path's presence.

Other acts of violence were directed at government and business institutions, symbols of the political and financial power that Shining Path was hoping to destroy. Terrorists firebombed courthouses and political party headquarters, including those of other less revolutionary left-wing organizations. Factories, mining operations, embassies, and banks were favorite targets of the guerrillas. So were churches; the Catholic hierarchy in Peru had traditionally aligned itself with the wealthy and powerful rather than with the poor.

The intensity and violence of these attacks, however, paled in comparison to the brutality of Shining Path's actions against the Peruvian people. At first, murder made up only a small part of the group's activities. During 1980, they killed three people—one landowner, one police officer, and one employee of a mining company. By 1982, approximately 130 people had died at the hands of Shining Path guerrillas. As the organization grew in strength, however, it became bolder and more brutal. Before long, it was indulging in wholesale slaughter of Peruvians.

"Those Who Refused Faced Death"

A number of these deaths were assassinations of particular civic leaders. The terrorists killed police officials in Lima and officers in the Peruvian armed forces. Shining Path also murdered many other left-wing radicals who did not share Guzman's revolutionary vision. One peaceful organizer in Lima, for instance, was shot in the head during a community meeting. Later, terrorists dynamited her corpse, sending an unmistakable message to those who had supported her.

The terrorists also murdered hundreds of prosecutors, mayors, and supervisors in the small towns and villages of central Peru. Most of these officials did little or nothing to irritate Shining Path guerrillas. Fearing the violence of the group, in fact, many of them went out of their way to avoid offending the

Andean villagers sit as army troops search the area for Shining Path guerrillas.

organization. According to the terrorists, though, these officials were supporting the government merely by holding government positions. Through violence like this, Shining Path came to control large stretches of the country.

But by far the greatest number of deaths were among ordinary villagers and farmers. Many of these Peruvians died in sudden and unexpected raids, often staged under the cover of darkness. "They came at night," reported one teenage girl in a town near Ayacucho. "[They] rounded up the women and told them there was no choice but to join the struggle. Those who refused faced death." [20]

The same basic outline was repeated in town after town. Thousands died on the spot. Many more joined the group with the intent of escaping as soon as possible, but escape often meant death when Guzman's troops caught up with the fugitives.

Shining Path guerrillas also entered towns by day, guns blazing. Many people were shot and killed while trying to run away from the terrorists. Others were dragged from hiding places and killed. This type of raid was most common in regions where Shining Path was at its strongest and feared little in the way of reprisals from government officials. Whether by day or by night, however, the result was usually the same: innocent civilians suffering violent deaths.

Purpose and Response

Of all Shining Path's violent acts, the attacks on poor farmers and villagers are perhaps the hardest to comprehend. The group's assassinations and many of their attacks on the nation's infrastructure had been designed to affect Shining Path's enemies: industry, government, and the wealthy of Peruvian society. But the villagers, as a rule, were hardly enthusiastic supporters of the state. And after all, Shining Path had been founded to protect and empower the poor.

The attacks took place regardless, and in at least one important way they were a natural outgrowth of Shining Path's philosophy and strategies. By waging violence against the poor, Shining Path's leaders terrified and controlled much of the Peruvian population. Wholesale murder of civilians served to silence even mild criticism of the group. In this way, Shining Path made it clear that there could be no neutrals. As members of the group saw it, people either supported the guerrillas wholeheartedly or they were considered to be in league with the hated opposition. Thus, a village could not feel safe from the marauders unless every single inhabitant of the place had pledged support to the terrorists.

Guzman also tended to encourage his followers to engage in all the violence they could. In his eyes, chaos would eventually lead to his goal of a stateless, classless, peaceful society. The faster the process, the sooner the new society would arrive. As a result,

even violence against the poor did not bother the guerrillas. "Violence is the only way," said a terrorist. "Innocent people always die, it's inevitable. Our task is to kill all those who stand in the way of Shining Path's war."[21] By 1992, most estimates agree, Shining Path had been responsible for the deaths of close to twenty-seven thousand people—many, probably most, guilty of nothing more than a failure to support the group to its satisfaction.

The violence had another purpose, too. By indulging in widespread terror, Shining Path hoped to bait the Peruvian government into establishing harsh antiterrorism measures. In this, the group succeeded. Peruvian leaders did strike back firmly. Presidents Alan Garcia and Alberto Fujimori both suspended constitutional rights in an effort to contain the

In 1992 Peruvian president Alberto Fujimori suspended the country's constitutional rights and dissolved its congress in an effort to contain the members and actions of Shining Path.

terror. Under both administrations, for example, suspected terrorists could be put in jail for extended periods of time without being officially charged with a crime and without coming to trial. Fujimori closed down the court system as well and even dissolved the Peruvian congress. The changes sparked irate protests from many Peruvians, who recognized that these measures affected innocent people as well as terrorists. Again, Guzman was aware that his message could best be heard if the government was alienated from the people.

Peruvian leaders also used military force that often matched Shining Path in its brutality and violence. One woman remembered the day government troops accused her family of helping the terrorists. Her family, she said, was innocent, but the soldiers did not believe them. "They cracked open my husband's head with a hammer," the woman reported, "and then with an ax they took out his brains."[22] As Guzman had hoped, such raids soured civilians on their government, especially when it became clear that many of those who died were innocent.

The violence was overblown and unnecessary, especially because government officials may have overestimated the terrorists' strength. Shining Path probably never had more than fifteen thousand active fighters, far from enough to take over a country. Nor did it have much in the way of resources. The guerrillas fought with relatively low-tech weapons. Most of their guns were old ones obtained from raids on army bases, and their dynamite was stolen from highway crews and mining corporations. Guzman received offers of aid from Communist groups outside Peru,

but he rejected them; by this time, Mao was dead, and no other Marxist leader met Guzman's standards for purity.

Nevertheless, the authorities were right to be concerned. The terrorists were an unusually tight-knit group of people who echoed Guzman's ideology and believed wholeheartedly in their cause. The relative lack of arms and numbers was outweighed by Shining Path's organization, strategy, and dedication. Guerrillas captured by government soldiers were rarely repentant. Instead, they painted pro-Guzman slogans on cell-block walls. "We are convinced that we will triumph," said one imprisoned terrorist, "and for that cause we are prepared to give our lives."[23]

Guzman in Charge

Since Shining Path's beginning, Guzman had been the spiritual and intellectual leader of the group. He directed its activities, shaped its ideology, and continued to eliminate party members who did not share his opinions. Now, however, the questioners were not simply kicked out of the party. They were murdered. No one was safe. In 1988, Guzman's wife Augusta supposedly committed suicide; however, some evidence suggests that she was forced into the act after a policy disagreement with her husband.

Guzman was a very shadowy presence after 1980. He lived entirely in hiding; he was always surrounded by bodyguards and moved secretly from one safe house to another. Guzman evaded detection so well that for many years virtually no one caught a glimpse of him, including many members of his own organization. For some time, in fact, police wondered whether he might be dead. The mystery added to Guzman's aura and made him seem more powerful than he really was.

But in August 1992, police received information that Guzman was living inside a house in a Lima residential neighborhood. Undercover agents confirmed that Guzman was in fact holed up in the house. On September 12, police sent several dozen antiterrorist agents into the neighborhood. So as not to attract attention, some were disguised as ice cream vendors or street peddlers. Many more were "guests" at a barbecue given by a police officer who happened to live nearby. One police couple parked a car across from the house, keeping an eye on the property while they kissed and drank beer. When the door to the house opened briefly, the couple in the car signaled the other agents. About thirty-five officers stormed inside, catching the terrorist leader and his bodyguards completely by surprise. Guzman put up no resistance and went peacefully to jail.

Trial and Reaction

The government was delighted to have captured Guzman, but the authorities handled him with extreme care. He was imprisoned on a small island off the Pacific coastline. The area around the island was declared off limits to all but military personnel, and Guzman was put under extremely heavy guard. Officials were worried that he might try to commit suicide or otherwise become a martyr to his cause. They also wanted to stop guerrillas from staging a dramatic rescue of their leader.

The next step was to bring Guzman to trial. Because of concerns that Shining Path

would attack participants, the trial was carried out in secrecy. The judges and prosecutors wore hoods to shield their identities, and no observers were allowed. Some questioned the fairness of the trial. But others defended the tight security and the safeguards. Shining Path's victims, after all, had included several judges who had sentenced guerrillas to prison. Moreover, many officials reasoned, a secret trial would give less attention to Shining Path.

It proved impossible to pin any individual murders on Guzman, but he was quickly found guilty of treason. The offense did not carry the death penalty, so he was sentenced to life imprisonment without the possibility of parole. Soon afterward, he was transferred to an underground isolation cell in another prison. The move, like the trial, was carried out in great secrecy. The crew of the ship that carried him wore hoods, and Guzman himself traveled inside a steel cage placed on the ship's deck.

As expected, the remaining Shining Path guerrillas were infuriated by their leader's capture and sentence. Many vowed to continue the struggle. "We will freeze your laughter, and don't complain," Shining Path members wrote in response to those who cheered Guzman's arrest. "Learn to suffer, learn to weep, learn to die."[24] For a while, attacks increased. Several police officers who had participated in the arrest were killed, and bombs went off throughout Lima on the day of the sentencing.

But without Guzman, the movement ultimately struggled. Shining Path's greatest strength had been its leader. Although

Guzman had not taken a direct role in most of the terrorist acts, he had given the guerrillas motivation and ideology. With him out of the picture, Shining Path had lost its heart and soul. Several people vied to take Guzman's place as leader, but in the end none could succeed. As one police officer put it, "Guzman was a god and ... no one would oppose him. There is no one now who can re-create that mystique."[25]

Over the next few years, Shining Path dwindled in members and influence. Many other guerrillas were caught and arrested. Still others quietly left the movement. In 1993, Guzman made an announcement from his prison cell, urging the remaining guerrillas to hammer out a peace agreement with government leaders. Some of the terrorists charged that Guzman was being tortured and had not made the statement of his own free will, but most experts saw no evidence of that. Without a leader, the movement was to all intents and purposes over, and Guzman's statements showed a recognition of that truth.

Guzman, surrounded by masked guards, is transferred to prison in a cage after receiving a life sentence for treason.

As of late 2001, Guzman remained imprisoned, confined to his underground cell nearly twenty-four hours a day. The organization he founded is still operating. From time to time, it continues to carry out terrorist acts, including a widely reported 1995 car bombing at a luxury hotel. But Guzman never appointed a successor, never allowed other members of the group to have a strong voice in planning and strategy, and never took an interest in encouraging political debate among his followers. In a very real way, the group was an extension of himself, held together through his authority and charismatic personality. When Guzman was arrested, Shining Path lost much of its reason for existence. Today, it is a rather marginal organization, hardly recognizable as the same group that spread terror across Peru for twelve tragic years.

Chapter Three

The Irish Republican Army

The Irish Republican Army (IRA) stands out in the history of terrorist organizations for its longevity, its organization, and its methods. It has been in existence far longer than almost any other group. Its origins date at least to 1916, and it has been in continued existence since then. The group is also significant because its story is not the story of any one or two important leaders. Instead, the IRA's activities have been the work of many individual people, no one of whom stands out as a mastermind of the whole organization.

Moreover, unlike many other terrorist factions, the IRA is not interested in political philosophy. The IRA does not try to promote a new form of government or try to push government leaders into becoming more liberal or conservative. Instead, the group defines itself in territorial and religious terms.

Its mission is to unite the six northeastern counties of Ireland, presently under British rule, with the remaining twenty-six counties that currently make up the Irish republic—a solution that is bitterly opposed by many in Northern Ireland and by a substantial number of those in the Irish republic as well.

Finally, the IRA is different from many other terrorist groups in that it takes some part in the political process. Whereas many terrorist organizations are content to spread violence, ignoring or sabotaging governmental operations, the IRA has often had a voice in legitimate political affairs. Over the years, a number of IRA members have run for and been elected to public office. Indeed, the IRA sprang in part from the success of a political party, which still exists today and functions as the political arm of the IRA.

The Roots of the IRA

The roots of the Irish Republican Army lie deep in Irish history. In comparison to England, its neighbor directly to the east, Ireland has always been a poor, rural, and relatively weak nation. As a result, it has been vulnerable to English rulers who have tried to take control of the island. These attempts began as early as the twelfth century, and continued on and off for about four hundred years.

Things became much worse during the sixteenth century, when King Henry VIII of England claimed all the land in Ireland as his own. Many Irish responded angrily, and Henry and his daughter Elizabeth I had to send English troops to Ireland several times to restore order. Making matters even more complex, Henry had founded his own Protestant church as the official religion of England, while the majority of Irish remained Roman Catholic. As a result, there was a religious difference between the Irish

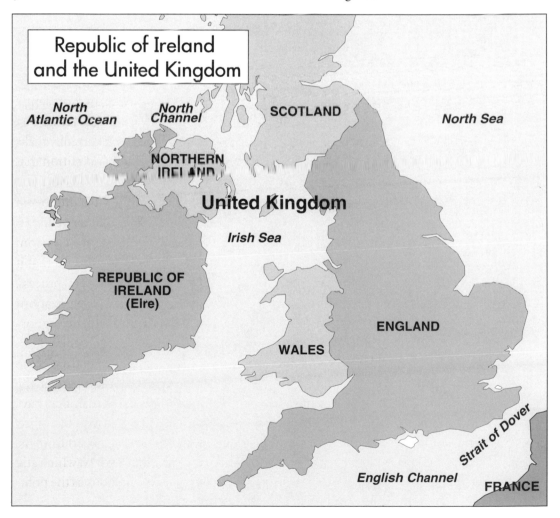

Republic of Ireland and the United Kingdom

North Atlantic Ocean

North Channel

SCOTLAND

North Sea

NORTHERN IRELAND

United Kingdom

Irish Sea

REPUBLIC OF IRELAND (Eire)

ENGLAND

WALES

English Channel

Strait of Dover

FRANCE

King James I wanted to establish a loyal Protestant group in Ireland and encouraged Protestants to settle there.

and the English as well as a cultural and ethnic one.

The situation worsened under the next English king, James I. James encouraged Scottish and English Protestants to move to Ireland. His objective was to create a loyal core of Protestants in Ireland, a group that would be supportive of England and its policies. In several northern counties, in fact, immigration was so great that the Protestants soon outnumbered the Catholics. However, the two groups did not accept each other. Fighting broke out, often bloody and occasionally brutal. Again and again, English troops came into the country to restore order—and to maintain control over the island for Britain.

Over the years, Irish Catholics came to despise the English and their interference in Irish affairs. Many generations continue to mourn tragic events in Irish history, often reliving them as though they had happened days, rather than centuries, before. The so-called flight of the earls in 1607, when several Catholic landholders left for France rather than submit to English rule, has been for years a vivid memory for many Irish Catholics. So has the campaign of 1649, in which the English ruler Oliver Cromwell put down an Irish rebellion with extreme violence. The events of 1688–1691, when King James II, a Catholic, tried and failed to regain the English throne from the Protestant king William of Orange, are also still prominent.

Irish Protestants, on the other hand, celebrated the events for which the Catholics grieved. While the Catholics put up portraits of James II in their houses, the Protestants posted pictures of William instead. The hostility between the groups intensified over time. Catholics and Protestants typically lived on separate sides of town and rarely interacted. When they did, it was usually to argue, to scuffle, and to throw stones at members of the other group. In the meantime, all of Ireland continued to be under the control of the English.

The Easter Rising

In 1914, World War I broke out in continental Europe, and England quickly joined in. With England's attention diverted, several patriotic Irish Catholic organizations took the opportunity to plan a revolt. The planners had some help from leaders of a minor political party known as Sinn Fein, a phrase meaning "ourselves" in Gaelic, the traditional language of Ireland.

The groups decided to carry out the revolt during Easter week of 1916. That Monday, armed men took control of a number of government buildings in Dublin, Ireland's largest city. The British sent in troops to put down the rebellion. Within the week, the British were once again in control. However, about thirteen hundred people had been killed in the fighting, and the British dealt harshly with those who took part in the Easter Rising. Police arrested hundreds of Catholics, some probably innocent of any wrongdoing, and executed more than a dozen of the revolt's leaders. For many Catholics, Britain's way of dealing with the situation was strongly reminiscent of Oliver Cromwell's campaign of 1649.

The Easter Rising thus did very little directly to change the situation in Ireland. But its impact was nevertheless widespread. Before the revolt, the organizations that had used violence to protest English rule had received little support from ordinary Irish Catholics. The Irish Citizens' Army, the Irish Republican Brotherhood, and similar groups were made up only of a few angry men who had struggled to recruit others to their point of view.

After the Easter Rising, though, things were very different. Furious with the English brutality, many Catholics took a renewed interest in Irish independence. Some of them expressed deep interest in joining one of the paramilitary organizations that had planned the rebellion. "If you strike us down now," proclaimed rebel Patrick Pearse shortly before facing the firing squad, "we shall rise again and renew the fight. You cannot conquer Ireland."[26]

Leaders of existing groups, however, decided that they would be best off banding together to form an entirely new organization to carry out acts of violence against the British. The task of creating this group fell to an Irishman named Michael Collins. A gregarious man who had spent time in prison

In 1919 Michael Collins became the leader of the newly formed Irish Republican Army.

for his work on behalf of Irish independence, Collins was among the leaders of the Irish Republican Brotherhood. He was a young man, not yet thirty, but he eagerly took on the responsibility of forming a new anti-England military force. Soon after the Easter Rising, the new group began to take shape. At first it was typically known as the Irish Volunteers, but by 1919 it had a new official name: the Irish Republican Army.

The time indeed turned out to be ripe for an effective paramilitary force. Sparked in part by the brutal British response to the Easter Rising, the IRA grew quickly, and its members were more committed than ever before. Before long, the IRA was much more powerful than any organization that had preceded it. Although many Irish Catholics still viewed it with suspicion, it nevertheless enjoyed far more popular support than any previous group.

Throughout 1917 and into 1918, IRA volunteers disrupted English rule in whatever way they could. They ambushed and murdered police officers. They spread out across the countryside on foot and by bicycle, bringing terror to English soldiers and supply centers. In some cases, they murdered Catholics they suspected of being informers for the British government. As one early IRA member argued, "All [who] assisted the enemy must be shot or otherwise destroyed with the least possible delay."[27]

Politics and Terror

The IRA was also strengthened greatly by its political connections. Ireland had had a voice in Britain's Parliament for many years. But before the Easter Rising took place, most Irish representatives had been committed to British rule; Irish nationalists had played only a small role in the government.

In the furor over British handling of the revolt, however, Irish nationalism moved into the political sphere. The small nationalist political party Sinn Fein, which had played a role in the planning of the Easter Rising, benefited especially. Many of Sinn Fein's members had been imprisoned by the British after the uprising, and a few had been killed. Still, the party won nearly all available Irish seats in the British elections of 1918, even though most of their candidates were in jail.

Simply capturing the seats, however, was not enough for Sinn Fein's leaders. Instead of taking their seats in London, those who were not in prison banded together and announced that they were forming a separatist Irish Parliament of their own. Their goal, the party's new legislators announced, was nothing short of Irish independence and the withdrawal of all English troops from the island.

As IRA leaders and Sinn Fein loyalists had expected, war soon broke out over the issue of Irish independence. The English quickly dissolved the new Irish Parliament altogether, although Sinn Fein members kept meeting in secret. Britain also upped the numbers of troops it stationed in Ireland. IRA members, in protest, stepped up their campaign of terror. The result was bloodshed, and plenty of it.

IRA commanders soon became legendary across Ireland for their raids on British soldiers and supplies. Michael Collins murdered fourteen British spies in one morning. In a 1920 ambush, IRA leader Tom Barry and his men killed eighteen English soldiers, burned two armored trucks, and made off with a large shipment of arms and ammunition. In another famous episode, Barry overcame a British ship as it lay in an Irish harbor.

Britain did not give in, however. Instead, it launched a campaign of terror of its own. A violent group of raiders, many drawn from the ranks of England's unemployed, spilled into Ireland. They destroyed property and injured or killed those who tried to resist. Like England's brutal response to the Easter Rising, the move backfired. Ordinary families with no IRA connections were forced off their land. Innocent civilians were shot in cold blood. Losing all sympathy for England, many of these men and women turned their support to the IRA.

The IRA members who died were viewed as martyrs. Eighteen-year-old medical student Kevin Barry, for example, became the subject of a popular patriotic song soon after he was put to death for his role in an ambush. The mayor of Cork, Terence MacSwiney, was arrested on questionable charges. He went on a hunger strike while in prison to call attention to the brutality of the English government. After seventy-four days without food, MacSwiney died of malnutrition. "I offer my pain for Ireland," he wrote shortly before his death. "I offer my suffering here for our martyred people." [28]

MacSwiney's sacrifice, like Kevin Barry's, galvanized Irish Catholics to the cause of Irish independence.

Peace—and More War

In 1921, after terrible violence on both sides, England and Ireland hammered out a peace treaty. The island would be divided into two parts. Most of the counties would band together to form a new nation, which would be called the Irish Free State. However, six heavily Protestant counties in the northeast would remain under British control; in these counties, the majority of citizens considered themselves British subjects. The system took effect in 1922. The compromise was acceptable to many Irish and English. Not only was it ratified by the Irish Parliament, it was even acceptable to many members of the IRA.

Still, some IRA members completely rejected the compromise. One reason was that the Irish Free State would not be entirely independent of Great Britain, rather, it would be a dominion, a self-governing country that owed allegiance to England. The other reason involved the northern counties, a region known as Ulster. A number of IRA members argued that British control of any part of the island—even a section dominated by Protestants—was unacceptable.

Thus, while men like Michael Collins laid down their arms after the signing of the peace treaty, others resolved to fight on. Under the leadership of Liam Lynch, the new chief of staff, the IRA continued to wage a campaign of terror in both Ulster and the Irish Free

Liam Lynch (third from right) and IRA leaders congregate after treaty talks in 1922.

State. Bombings, shootings, and ambushes were regular occurrences on both sides of the border. Through the spring of 1923, people on both sides died in fighting at the rate of more than three hundred a month.

The IRA was by no means responsible for all of the violence, but it played a very large role in beginning and continuing it. According to its 1922 constitution, the group's main objective was to unite all of Ireland—including the majority Protestant sections of the island—under a common Catholic banner, completely independent of England. IRA members were quite willing to use violent means to achieve this goal. Those

means included assassination. In August 1922, Michael Collins was shot and killed by his former friends, and other onetime IRA members suffered similar fates.

Continuing the Struggle

By now, though, the militants did not enjoy as much popular support as before. Many Irish Catholics, especially in the south, simply wanted peace. They were happy enough with the treaty as it stood. A group of Catholic bishops issued a statement decrying the violence. "[IRA members] have caused more damage to Ireland in three months," they wrote, "than could be laid to the charge of

British rule in [as] many decades."[29] In a fine example of shifting alliances, Britain actually helped arm the Irish Free State, a former bitter enemy, because now both were working against the terrorists.

The anti-IRA efforts nearly succeeded. By the middle of 1923, the IRA had lost most of its leaders. Some were killed outright in fighting. Liam Lynch, for example, was ambushed and mortally wounded. Others were captured and put to death. With the odds heavily against the rebels, former IRA member Eamon De Valera urged the remaining guerrillas to give up the armed struggle for peaceful means. Most of the IRA men still in the field agreed. For a time, incidents of violence diminished considerably.

But IRA terror did not entirely disappear. Throughout the 1920s, remaining IRA members occasionally raided police stations, shot men suspected of being police informers, and blew up buildings associated with the English government. Some of the tensions were further eased in the 1930s, when the Irish Free State ceased to be a dominion and became instead a thoroughly independent Republic of Ireland. However, the continued existence of a separate Northern Ireland under British control distressed a few Irish nationalists, who kept up a campaign of terror concentrated mainly in Ulster.

In 1939, the IRA made a change in strategy: Its operatives began to carry the campaign of violence to England itself. To carry out this plan, IRA terrorists traveled inconspicuously to Great Britain. There they placed bombs in marketplaces and government buildings. That spring and summer, there were well over 150 different explosions. The overall death toll was not especially large—the worst explosion killed only five—but the psychological cost and the property damage were enormous.

A New Wave of Terror

Still, for the period, the wave of bombings in England was an exception. In general, IRA terror remained at a relatively low level from 1923 to the middle of the 1960s, when tensions began to increase once more in Ulster. The troubles began when members of Northern Ireland's Catholic minority, upset at unfair treatment by British officials, started a series of protests modeled in part on the U.S. civil rights movement.

The Catholics in Ulster were the victims of prejudice, and the bias they experienced was not all that different from what African Americans of the time went through in the South. There was widespread discrimination against Ulster Catholics in jobs and housing well into the 1960s, and the political system was biased against Catholics as well. The Protestant majority was clearly in charge in the region. "All I boast is that we are a Protestant parliament and a Protestant state,"[30] said Ulster government leader James Craig in the 1930s; that sort of attitude was still prevalent more than thirty years later.

In October 1968, Catholic leaders planned a protest march for an Ulster town known to Catholics as Derry and to Protestants as Londonderry. The British government, fearing that the march would turn violent, banned the protest. The marchers decided to ignore the ruling. They had barely started on their

People of Broadgate, England, examine the destruction caused by an IRA bomb in 1939.

journey when they were viciously attacked by a Protestant paramilitary force. In response, Catholic demonstrations against the situation in Ulster increased, with similar reprisals by Protestants. In 1969, conditions had deteriorated so badly that Northern Ireland officials called in the British army to help restore order.

Some Catholics supported this move; after all, it was mostly Catholics who were being hurt, and many believed that the police might provide protection for the marchers. Even a few longtime IRA members welcomed the presence of the army, as long as it was temporary. But others were unconvinced. Just as it had split in response to the 1920s peace treaty, the IRA now split over its

response to the situation. One group, now called the Official IRA, determined to peacefully support the Catholic protesters. The other group—the Provisional IRA, or the Provos for short—decided to meet the Protestants' tactics with terror of its own.

By 1970, IRA violence in Northern Ireland had reached levels unknown since the early 1920s. "The basic idea was to blow police stations away," remembered one terrorist affiliated with the Provos. "What the IRA literally did was to walk up to [a police station], hang a five-pound bomb on the door, light the fuse and run away."[31] The new IRA also attacked civilians. On one occasion, when heavily armed Protestant marchers converged on a Catholic section of Ulster,

IRA members shot the leaders of the march as they entered Catholic "territory." In the ensuing melee, several Protestants died and many more were injured.

Foreign Ties

Just as it had during the time of the Easter Rising, the IRA received—and deserved—a large share of the credit for attempting to fight off British troops and Ulster Protestants during the 1970s. Likewise, IRA violence again sparked a backlash from the organization's enemies. The British soldiers and the anti-Catholic marchers once more came down overly harshly on Catholics. They smashed houses and beat people almost at random. All of this brutality led to widespread resentment and to more, not less, support for the IRA.

But support at home was not enough. The IRA had plenty of men and plenty of backing from the Catholics of Northern Ireland; what it needed now was weapons, and money with which to buy them. IRA members received cash, arms, and support from a number of countries, most of whom gave in secret. South Africa, for instance, gave extensive support to the Irish terrorists. So did several Middle Eastern groups, notably Palestinian rebels who offered training in terror techniques, and Muammar Qaddafi of Libya, who mostly provided weapons. The reasons why these groups helped are unclear.

The largest contributions, however, came from private citizens in the United States. Millions of Catholic Irish Americans in Chicago, Boston, New York, and other cities were eager to support the Irish cause. Many knew the proud tales of Irish resistance and wanted to help establish a free and united Ireland. IRA operatives canvased these Irish Americans. Sometimes they were quite clear that the Americans' support would lead to purchases of weapons. On other occasions, they were deliberately vague, indicating only that contributions would be used for the goal of a united Ireland. Support from foreign citizens, groups, and governments helped turn the IRA into a strong, resourceful—and vicious—fighting machine.

Brutality

To be sure, the IRA did not generally see itself as brutal. IRA leaders such as Sean MacStiofain, the chief of staff for the group in the early 1970s, insisted that the IRA inflicted terror only in response to the violence of the British army and the Ulster Protestants. Moreover, MacStiofain and others argued, the IRA damaged property rather than human beings. "Every time the British army attacked our people," said another Ulster commander, Billy McKee, "we got [IRA] Volunteers into the center of town and set bombs off there. . . . It was done in places where there was practically no civilians about, you know. And we always gave notification."[32]

McKee and MacStiofain were partly right. The other side absolutely had its excesses. In one particularly appalling case, a Protestant group known as the Shankill Butchers tortured, killed, and dismembered nineteen or more Catholics over a period of several years. And British troops often were extremely quick to fire their guns. Without such behavior, it is certainly possible that the

IRA leader Sean MacStiofain rises to speak at a press conference that was part of IRA peace talks.

IRA might not have been so brutal in its treatment of the enemy.

Still, the IRA could be just as vindictive, perhaps even more so. In one case, IRA members lured three unarmed reserve soldiers into a car and killed them with shots to the back of the head, sparking a wave of disgust even among many Catholics. In another case, IRA operatives booby-trapped a car belonging to a suspected member of a Protestant military group, killing him and his daughter and seriously injuring his baby. After yet another attack, IRA members justified the

bombing of a hospital by arguing that British soldiers were on the grounds.

The IRA policed its own, too. Young Catholic women who spent time with British soldiers or with Protestants were beaten or tarred and feathered by angry IRA operatives. Similarly, those suspected of spying for the enemy were often shot in the knee, giving the victim a permanent limp or eliminating his ability to walk altogether. "You have to be very bad to be shot in the knee," argued one IRA source, "and if you are very, very bad, you are shot in the kneecaps and elbows."[33] There is evidence that some informers were killed, as well.

Events in England

During the 1970s, the IRA spread terror in England, too, just as it had done several decades earlier. This time, however, technological advances and foreign aid provided the group with more lethal explosives, and the IRA was also better equipped to carry out its activities. IRA members set off bombs in pubs, restaurants, and other public places. Harrod's department store in London was bombed, as was the London Stock Exchange. In 1979, a bomb went off in a boat belonging to a British nobleman, Lord Louis Mountbatten, who died instantly.

The IRA made headlines with other actions, too. During the 1970s, many IRA terrorists were captured by British armed forces and brought to prisons in England and Northern Ireland. Hoping to be seen as political prisoners, these men asked for special treatment from their jailers. For instance, they wanted to wear their own clothing rather than prison uniforms, and they asked for recreational and educational opportunities forbidden to those put in jail for other reasons.

The British government did at one point agree to some of these demands, on the condition that the IRA stop its violence. But the agreement soon fell apart, and Britain revoked the special treatment. In 1980, several IRA members in Ulster prisons followed

Harrod's department store was one of many public places that were bombed in London during the 1970s.

in the footsteps of Terence MacSwiney by staging a hunger strike to protest the British decision. The strike was short-lived, but the following year a number of prisoners tried again. British officials decided against force feeding the men as they slowly lost weight. But they also made it clear that they would not accede to the prisoners' demands.

Several protesters did give up their fasts, but ten did not and ultimately died of starvation. "The body fights back, sure enough," said Bobby Sands, an IRA activist who was the first of the prisoners to die, "but at the end of the day, everything returns to the mind."[34] As had MacSwiney and other earlier Irish rebels, these IRA members had resolved to die for what they perceived to be a greater good: the uniting of Ireland and the expulsion of British influence. Indeed, the use of hunger as a means of protest was quite deliberate; it attempted to draw a straight line between the earlier struggles of Irish Catholics against English rule and the situation in the 1980s.

Today

The hunger strikes ended in the early 1980s, but IRA terror continued through that decade and well into the next. The history of the IRA since 1980 has been quite similar to the organization's history in earlier years. As before, operatives destroyed bridges, planted car bombs, and assassinated those who got in their way. In 1996, for example, a van exploded near the city center of Manchester, England, injuring two hundred people and causing millions of dollars in property damage. Similarly, in 1998 a bomb in Omagh, Northern Ireland, killed twenty-nine people, including a number of children.

Justification for the violence remains the same, too. The leaders of the group, such as Mickey McKevitt, brother-in-law of hunger strike casualty Bobby Sands, continue to draw on old themes in explaining the group's commitment to terror. In particular, IRA members cite the long-standing British oppression of Irish Catholics and British brutality in putting down rebellions in the early and middle parts of the twentieth century. Their primary goal is the same as well: a united Ireland.

Over time, the IRA has continued to undergo changes and splits. Just as in the past, some IRA members give up the armed struggle or join the IRA's political wing when peace seems to be a real possibility. Gerry Adams,

Gerry Adams was an IRA terrorist and is now head of Sinn Fein, an organization looking to find political solutions to the problems of Northern Ireland.

Children run past graffiti indicating that some factions of the IRA may be willing to decommission, or put down, their weapons in support of Northern Ireland's 2000 peace agreement.

for example, was an IRA terrorist as a young adult. During the early 1970s, he was imprisoned and beaten, and British officials told his family that he was dead. Today, he is the head of Sinn Fein, a legitimate political figure trying to find a political solution to the problems in Northern Ireland—although many Protestants continue to view him with deep suspicion. Another former terrorist, Martin McGuinness, later became Northern Ireland's minister for education.

At the same time, several splinter groups have formed from factions of the IRA. Frustrated with the slow pace of change and afraid that political solutions will betray the Ulster Catholics, these groups have stepped up the violence. Most recently, a group calling itself the True IRA has spun off from the regular guerrilla army; it was this group that

claimed responsibility for the 1998 bombing in Omagh. This blast—and similar ones—kept up the pace of terror that has marked Ulster for several generations and left more than three thousand dead since 1968.

Nevertheless, the various sides in the conflict have made some progress toward establishing a peace treaty. In 1997, the IRA accepted a temporary cease-fire agreement while peace talks took place. The talks culminated in a tentative agreement among politicians to share power in Northern Ireland among all those who would commit to nonviolence. This deal became known as the Good Friday accord, and it represented a major step in the direction of peace: Sinn Fein and the Irish republic agreed to recognize some of Britain's claims to the region—claims based mainly on the fact that a majority of Ulster residents consider themselves British subjects—and British loyalists put a stop to some of the most overt acts of anti-Catholic prejudice. The agreement was ratified by a large majority of Northern Ireland voters in May 1998.

The peace process is not over yet. In 2000, some Protestant groups withdrew from the Good Friday treaty on the grounds that the IRA had not yet fully disarmed. Hostilities and suspicions still linger, evidenced most recently by name-calling and stone-throwing aimed at schoolchildren in September 2001. More than one observer has noted that while Ulster has plenty of Catholics and plenty of Protestants, it has a severe shortage of Christians.

Ulster remains a battle-scarred place, a section of the world with high unemployment and widespread poverty. Disaffected Protestants and Catholics alike still find it easy to blame the other side for their own people's troubles; some still find it tempting to resort to violence. The history of the region remains a source of conflict for both sides, and the influence of the IRA and its Protestant counterparts is far from ended. Still, there are signs that the worst of the violence in Northern Ireland may be over.

Chapter Four

Timothy McVeigh

On April 19, 1995, a bomb exploded outside the Alfred P. Murrah Federal Building in Oklahoma City. The blast ripped an enormous hole in the front half of the building, which housed government offices and a day care center. Although rescuers were able to save a number of people from the destruction, 168 people died, making the attack the worst terrorist action on American soil at the time. At first, most people assumed that the attack was the work of Muslim extremists, but in fact the truth lay a good deal closer to home.

Within two days, the police had arrested a young American named Timothy McVeigh and charged him with the crime. The arrest was a surprise to many who had known McVeigh. A former soldier who had served with distinction during the Persian Gulf War, McVeigh was regarded as a patriotic American who cared deeply for his country. He had grown up in a middle-class family, he had done well in school, and he had never been in trouble with the law. In all these ways, McVeigh seemed an unlikely candidate to be a terrorist.

Timothy McVeigh masterminded the 1995 bombing of the federal building in Oklahoma City.

McVeigh was nevertheless guilty. His act of terror was sparked by an extreme antigovernment perspective. Beginning in his high school days, McVeigh had been drawn to a deeply conservative, or right-wing, political philosophy, the centerpiece of which was a distrust of the federal government. As McVeigh grew older, the distrust turned into a conviction that the U.S. government was a great evil. In his view, the government was infringing on Americans' rights and needed to be stopped. At Oklahoma City that April morning, Timothy McVeigh put his ideas into practice.

Growing Up

Timothy McVeigh was born on April 23, 1968, in Lockport, a town in the western part of New York. He grew up there and in the smaller nearby town of Pendleton. McVeigh's father, Bill, was a factory worker; his mother, Mickey, took a job as a travel agent several years after Timothy's birth. The couple also had two girls: Patty, two years older than Timothy, and Jennifer, who was born in 1974.

Growing up, Timothy McVeigh had a number of friends among the local children. "I hung around with a bunch of kids in the neighborhood," he remembered years later. "We'd go hiking quite a bit in the backwoods."[35] During the summers, he played youth baseball, swam, and rode his bicycle; in the winter, he went ice skating. McVeigh also did well in elementary school; his teachers appreciated his hard work and cooperative attitude.

McVeigh's high school years also seemed uneventful. Teachers remembered him as a good student who did not always work to his full potential. He got a job at a local fast food restaurant, and he developed a strong interest in comic books, purchasing old and rare issues for investment purposes. Around school, he was known for talking all the time; his graduating class voted him the most talkative senior.

There were problems within McVeigh's family, however. With both parents working demanding and intensive jobs, McVeigh was usually on his own as a child. "I have very few memories . . . of interaction with my parents," he said in an interview. "I was often by myself or with neighbors."[36] When McVeigh turned ten, his parents' marriage broke up. The children were asked to choose where they wanted to live. Timothy's sisters chose to move to Florida with their mother, while Timothy stayed in Pendleton with his father.

There were other undercurrents of possible problems as well. In high school, McVeigh's greatest interest was guns. He spent hours shooting at cans he set up in the woods. He also spent time poring through gun magazines and catalogs. Still, this interest did not seem to indicate any particular concerns: Many boys of the same age have been interested in guns, and McVeigh never used his rifle to shoot anything other than cans.

Somewhat more unusual was McVeigh's interest in survivalism. Many of the weapons magazines he read warned of approaching disaster. Some projected a possible World War III. They urged their readers to build bomb shelters, stock up on food and water, and gather weapons to prepare themselves for disaster. McVeigh took the warnings seriously. He stored gunpowder and huge barrels of water in his basement. After high school, he and a friend bought a parcel of undeveloped land together. "He wanted to build a bomb shelter there," said the friend. "He was afraid of nuclear war."[37]

The Military

After high school graduation, McVeigh briefly attended a business college, but dropped out; he was tired of school. Instead, he got a permit to carry a loaded handgun and went to work as a security guard. McVeigh enjoyed the work and was good at it. However, he was not particularly well paid, and after a while he found himself yearning for less routine and more action. In 1988, twenty years old, McVeigh enlisted in the army.

McVeigh became an enthusiastic and committed soldier. He was sent to Georgia for basic training and then to Kansas for infantry school.

In both places, he demonstrated intelligence, hard work, and determination. He spent most of his free time cleaning his weapons in the barracks. McVeigh also became an excellent marksman; on several occasions, he achieved perfect scores in tests of accuracy.

McVeigh rose quickly through the ranks. Before long, he had achieved the title of sergeant. Throughout his training, he was well respected and admired by his superior officers. His fellow soldiers respected him as well, though they did not always understand the enthusiasm he brought to his tasks. The army was a good fit, and McVeigh knew it. He would be a career army officer, he told friends; he had found his niche.

In 1990, the Gulf War broke out in the Middle East. Iraq attacked Kuwait, and the

Two U.S. soldiers look over the remains of an Iraqi SCUD missile that was shot down during the Gulf War.

following January, after issuing several warnings, the United States came to Kuwait's defense. McVeigh traveled to Saudi Arabia with his unit, where he served as a gunner. He rode atop an armored troop transport and shot a cannon at enemy troops. The job was difficult and demanding, but McVeigh excelled at the task. For his hard work he received a medal.

McVeigh found much to dislike about the war with Iraq, however. He believed that the U.S. military should not be helping to defend allies, but should only be protecting America itself. The United States, he noted, was not directly threatened by Iraq before or during the war. More specifically, McVeigh also worried about the ethics of killing people for whom he felt no personal anger. "These were human beings," he said later, "even though they speak a different language and have different customs." [38]

Nevertheless, McVeigh returned to the United States after the war eager to continue his military work. He hoped to become a member of the army's elite special forces squad, a group of highly trained soldiers who carry out dangerous operations. But McVeigh failed the entrance exam when he dropped out halfway through a long march. McVeigh blamed blisters caused by stiff new boots, but

McVeigh, pictured here in uniform, was a gunner for the U.S. Army during the Gulf War.

he also blamed the timing: During the Gulf War, he had had little opportunity to keep himself in good condition.

Danger Signs

Some observers have asserted that McVeigh failed not only the physical exam but also a psychological test given to would-be special forces members. (The army has not commented on this allegation.) It is certainly true that by the conclusion of the Gulf War, McVeigh's interest in survivalism and weapons had gone off in new and unsettling directions. Despite his undeniable military skills, some of his fellow soldiers worried about his emotional stability.

During his years in the army, McVeigh often read extremely conservative publications that strongly criticized the federal government. Many of these newsletters and magazines were published by the militia movement, a loose organization of right-wing gun owners interested in survivalism and protecting the right to bear arms. The publications mostly warned that the national government was trying to take away guns from law-abiding citizens.

However, the editors of these magazines and newsletters spoke out on issues besides guns, too. Many argued, for example, that the United States was being overrun by racial minorities and immigrants; that American property rights were in serious jeopardy; and that the United States was ceding its power to international bodies like the United Nations. Some advocated rebellion against the government in the form of not paying taxes or refusing to recognize federal authority. A few went further; they suggested armed violence.

McVeigh soon came to agree that the federal government was not a friend to the people. His perspective was strengthened after reading a novel called *The Turner Diaries*. Written by a former American Nazi Party official, *The Turner Diaries* combined racism, survivalism, and antigovernment thought. It told of a small group of patriotic white supremacist gun owners standing up to an evil federal government. In the military, McVeigh read the novel many times and loaned it to all his friends.

Increasingly, McVeigh's companions shared his worldview. In the military, he had developed a friendship with a Michigan resident named Terry Nichols. He had also gotten to know Michael Fortier, a soldier from Arizona. Both Nichols and Fortier came to the military with political perspectives similar to McVeigh's. McVeigh shared his own ideas with these two men; he also learned more about the world of extreme right-wing politics from them.

Ruby Ridge and Waco

McVeigh left the military in late 1991, soon after being rejected for special forces. Returning to the Buffalo area, he resumed working security for a time. He also worked part-time at a local gun store. Over the next several months, his anger toward the federal government grew as he pondered the messages of *The Turner Diaries* and the other ultraconservative publications he had read. He engaged fellow security guards, family members, and friends in political discussions.

During his testimony on Capitol Hill, Randy Weaver holds up his door that was shot by federal agents.

He made claims that some recalled as bizarre, arguing at one point that the government was building concentration camps and crematoriums to kill and imprison those Americans unwilling to sacrifice their rights.

McVeigh's distrust of the federal government was soon reinforced. In August 1992, federal agents raided the home of white separatist Randy Weaver in Ruby Ridge, Idaho. Accused of violating weapons laws, Weaver fought back. In the resulting gun battle, Weaver's son and wife were killed; a U.S. marshal died as well. McVeigh, like many others on the far right, thought the incident demonstrated the brutality of the federal government.

In early 1993, a similar incident took place when government agents surrounded a compound in Waco, Texas. The compound belonged to a religious cult known as the Branch Davidians; like Randy Weaver, the Branch Davidians were suspected of possessing illegal weaponry. Despite being surrounded, the cult refused to give up. But the government would not give in, either, and the siege went on for several weeks.

McVeigh, again, was appalled. In his view, the government was harassing innocent people for daring to assert their constitutional right to own weapons. McVeigh visited Waco, where he sold bumper stickers bearing antigovernment slogans. "The government is continually growing bigger and more powerful," he told a reporter, "and the people need to defend themselves against government control." [39]

The Waco siege ended on April 19 when the agents set fire to the compound, killing many who were inside. Many mainstream Americans saw Waco as an example of excessive federal use of force. That was even more true among those on the far right, and McVeigh was no exception. If McVeigh had been angry at government actions before, now he was furious. The attack on Waco was a turning point in his life.

"Blood Will Flow in the Streets"

After Waco, McVeigh's rhetoric became increasingly radical. He drifted from town to town, supporting himself largely by selling merchandise at gun shows. He stayed for a while with Michael Fortier in Arizona. He also visited Terry Nichols at his new home in Kansas, and he spent time at the Nichols family farm in Michigan. More and more, McVeigh's talk turned to violence. "Blood will flow in the streets," he wrote in a letter to a childhood acquaintance. "Good vs. evil, freemen vs. socialist wannabe slaves. Pray it is not your blood, my friend." [40]

Sometime during these travels, McVeigh's talk began to turn to action, and over the next

The compound in Waco, Texas, burns after the fifty-one day standoff between the Branch Davidians and the F.B.I.

two years a plan began to take shape in his mind. He decided to carry out a violent strike against the government itself, and he chose as his target the Alfred P. Murrah Federal Building in Oklahoma City. To McVeigh, the building was a symbol of the federal government's influence. McVeigh also believed—erroneously—that the Murrah Building was home base to some of the federal agents involved in the Waco incident.

McVeigh selected April 19, 1995, as the date of the bombing. April 19 had plenty of significance for McVeigh. For one, it marked the anniversary of the attack at Waco. For another, it was the date of the Battle of Lexington, the opening engagement of the Revolutionary War; McVeigh and other supporters of the militia movement patterned themselves after the American patriots who had stood up to the power of a corrupt British government. To McVeigh, carrying out his terrorist action on April 19 would show solidarity with colonial fighters while also avenging the Branch Davidians.

McVeigh planned carefully and secretively. He got help from Fortier and Nichols; beyond that, he seems to have worked more or less independently. McVeigh knew he could manufacture a large and powerful explosive from fertilizer, race-car fuel, blasting caps, and other relatively ordinary materials. He gathered these materials under assumed names, paying cash and attracting as little attention as possible. Most likely, McVeigh and Nichols actually put the bomb together at a state park in Kansas a few days before April 19.

Transportation was easy, too. On April 17, McVeigh rented a yellow moving van from an agency in Junction City, Kansas. Again, he paid cash and used a fake name. McVeigh also bought an old Mercury Marquis to serve as his getaway vehicle. He and Nichols drove separately to Oklahoma City. McVeigh parked the Marquis a few blocks from the Murrah Building. Then they both headed back to Kansas in Nichols's car.

The Blast

Around nine o'clock on Wednesday morning, April 19, Timothy McVeigh parked his rented truck in front of the Murrah Building. The bomb sat in the back of the truck, ready for detonation. McVeigh had chosen a time for the explosion that he hoped would maximize the number of people in the building. Since property damage was not his goal, he had no desire to set off a blast with the building empty. For McVeigh to make his point, innocent people would have to die.

For McVeigh, there was no questioning the morality of his decision. In his view, he was engaged in a war against the government, and war did not follow ordinary ethical principles. Even the presence of children in a day care center did not dissuade him. McVeigh drew a parallel with the bombing of Iraq during Desert Storm. "The administration has admitted to knowledge of the presence of children in or near Iraqi government buildings," he wrote afterward, "yet they still proceed with their plans to bomb—saying they cannot be held responsible if children die. . . . Who are the true barbarians?"[41]

The front of the federal building in Oklahoma City was obliterated after McVeigh's bomb exploded.

McVeigh lit the fuse and left the truck as quickly as he could without attracting attention. At 9:02, the bomb exploded. Instantly, the front of the nine-story office building sheared off and smashed into a pile of rubble. Damage to the rear of the building was extensive, too. All over downtown Oklahoma City, buildings shook. Plate glass rained down from windows. Flying pieces of metal and concrete filled the air. The sound of the blast could be heard miles away.

The entire building did not collapse, however, and many people, though injured, made it safely out back entrances. Rescue crews hurried to the scene of the disaster. Working as hard as they could and in extremely cramped conditions, they managed to save several dozen people who had been trapped in the wreckage. But over five hundred people were hurt, many critically so.

It was clear from the beginning that the death toll would be high. Many people had died instantly in the blast. The collapse of part of the building and the flying projectiles had killed many more. Others bled to death when rescue workers could not reach them in time. In all, the terrorist attack on the Murrah Building killed 168 people: 163 inside the building; 4 on the street or in nearby buildings; and 1 who died while helping the rescue efforts. Nineteen of the dead were children.

Arrest

While rescue workers poured into Oklahoma City, McVeigh headed north for Kansas in his Marquis. Near the town of Perry, however, he was pulled over by an Oklahoma state trooper, who had noticed that McVeigh's car lacked a rear license plate. McVeigh was heavily armed and later told a reporter that he considered killing the trooper. He did not, however, perhaps because the man was a state rather than a federal employee. The trooper placed him under arrest on weapons charges and brought him to the county jail. He spent two nights there while awaiting a hearing.

McVeigh expected to be released on bail. He had no criminal record, he was clean-cut and courteous, and there was nothing in his arrest to connect him with the bombing in Oklahoma City. In any case, no one was looking for a white American terrorist. Authorities and the general public believed at first that the bombing was the work of Middle Eastern radicals. In fact, there were reports of assaults committed against Muslims around the country immediately after the bombing.

Authorities soon discovered, though, that the Middle Eastern connection was wrong. McVeigh had anticipated that the explosion would incinerate his rental van, but by a fluke, it did not. One piece of the truck's axle survived the blast. The van's vehicle identification number had been etched on the axle, and some of it was still readable. A quick trace of the number revealed that the van belonged to the agency in Junction City.

McVeigh had used an assumed name, Robert Kling, to rent the van, but the staff at the agency remembered McVeigh well enough to provide a general description.

Federal agents canvased the area with rough sketches of "Kling," looking for more information. A local motel owner soon identified the man in the picture as one of her guests, and McVeigh had inadvertently checked in to the motel under his real name. When the police did a routine computer check of people currently in custody around the state, they were shocked to discover that the man they sought was in the Perry jail. From there, getting McVeigh into federal custody was easy.

The Trial

McVeigh's trial was moved to Colorado because of concerns that an Oklahoma jury would be biased against him. His friends Nichols and Fortier were arrested, too, and tried separately for their roles in the terrorist attack. McVeigh, however, was tried first. Jury selection began in March 1996.

The evidence against McVeigh was strong. There was no doubt that he had rented the truck. At the other end, several witnesses agreed that they had seen him drive up to the Murrah Building that day. Laboratory tests revealed traces of bomb materials on McVeigh's clothing. He had purchased large quantities of fertilizer (which was one of the ingredients used in making the bomb) before the attack, and Fortier and his wife both said they had heard McVeigh talk about blowing up government property.

Despite the evidence, McVeigh pleaded not guilty. His attorney, Stephen Jones, tried to cast doubt on several elements of the government's story. Jones pointed out, for example, that no one had actually seen McVeigh construct the bomb. Still, the jury was not convinced. On June 2, 1997, they found McVeigh guilty of murder. Eleven days later, they condemned him to death. Many survivors were delighted, but McVeigh found the sentence illogical. "I was accused and convicted of killing," he said. "Now they're going to kill me.... They're saying that's an appropriate way to right a wrong?"[42]

McVeigh replaced Jones with a new legal team and launched a series of appeals. He argued that the judge had unfairly excluded witnesses who might have helped his case.

He also argued that the jury pool was tainted because several jurors had erroneously heard that McVeigh had confessed to his lawyers. Still, McVeigh held out little hope for a successful appeal. "Because of the intense public pressure and demand for my blood," he wrote in a letter to a newspaper, "I do not see an appeals court ruling in my favor."[43] In September, a federal appellate court did indeed reject his initial appeal, and in March 1999, the U.S. Supreme Court also refused to overturn the verdict.

Prosecuters for the Oklahoma City bombing cheer after hearing the guilty verdict of McVeigh.

McVeigh and his lawyers pore over evidence in an effort to delay his execution.

"It Was a Military Action"

Death sentences in the United States are often delayed for months or even years while lawyers explore ways of overturning either the verdict or the sentence. But in December 2000, McVeigh instructed his lawyers to drop the appeals. His execution was then set for May 2001. Early that month, however, evidence arose that the FBI had not let McVeigh's lawyers see important documents pertaining to the trial. McVeigh briefly decided to fight for another trial on the basis of this information, but gave up the notion when it became clear that the documents contained nothing that would lead to a new verdict.

On June 11, after a last meal of mint chocolate chip ice cream, Timothy McVeigh was given a lethal injection for planning and carrying out what ranked at the time as the worst terrorist attack on U.S. territory. He died early that morning, mostly unapologetic. "He wishes to make it known that he does feel for people," said one of his lawyers. "But again, that is not to say that he thinks he was wrong. In his mind, it was a military action." [44] Although McVeigh did have co-conspirators (both Terry Nichols and Michael Fortier received jail sentences for their roles in the bombing), he alone was the driving force behind the disaster. In the long run, McVeigh was proof that terrorism does not require a large group of fighters to be successful. Mass destruction can result from the actions of one disaffected human being. The Oklahoma City bombing demonstrated how easily a single person could create terror in a place where no one expected to see it.

Chapter Five

Osama bin Laden and al-Qaeda

F ew terrorists have been as danger-ous as Osama bin Laden. A wealthy and educated Muslim originally from Saudi Arabia, bin Laden spent many years creating a network of terrorists designed to spread violence around the globe. His ideas, funds, and personali-ty all helped inspire people to join his organization, which he called al-Qaeda—an Arabic term meaning "the base." Both founder and leader of al-Qaeda, bin Laden has masterminded some of the most vicious terrorist attacks ever recorded.

Bin Laden and his group are dan-gerous because they are quite powerful and well organized. Al-Qaeda is an organization rich in members, exper-tise, and commitment to a cause. It has operatives worldwide, most of them with a fierce loyalty to their leader as well as his ideals. Bin Laden has taken advantage of this loyalty to carry out a wide range of attacks. Few other ter-rorist leaders have a similar following; likewise, few have the money, the weaponry, and the know-how enjoyed by al-Qaeda. This strong base has enabled bin Laden to carry out acts of terror beyond the capacity of many other terrorist leaders.

Bin Laden's status as perhaps the most feared terrorist on earth also stems, in part, from his choice of tar-gets. Although bin Laden's first attacks were concentrated on Middle Eastern countries, the real focus of his anger lay elsewhere. A staunch opponent of American political and military poli-cies, bin Laden intended his Middle Eastern attacks to hurt Americans and their allies. Moreover, while most other terrorist groups confine their activities to a relatively small geographic area, bin Laden's hatred for the United States has led him to stage attacks in many

Osama bin Laden has planned some of the world's most menacing terrorist attacks.

Elusive, powerful, and angry: This is Osama bin Laden. His insistence on secrecy enabled him to create al-Qaeda without attracting attention from the rest of the world; his anger at the United States attracted like-minded Muslims, who offered him money, weapons, and soldiers. Given bin Laden's resources, his fury, and his ability to hide, perhaps it is no surprise that he became one of the most menacing terrorists in history.

Early Years

Much remains unclear about the shape of Osama bin Laden's life. What information does exist is scanty and often questionable; sources frequently conflict with one another, and details are often lacking. Because of this, bin Laden's biography contains significant gaps. It is difficult, for instance, to say with any certainty what influences bin Laden had in developing his political philosophy, and much about the founding and structure of al-Qaeda remains almost completely unknown.

Osama bin Laden was born in 1957 to an enormously wealthy Saudi contractor, Mohammed Awad bin Laden. He was one of over fifty brothers and sisters born to the elder bin Laden and his many wives. His parents were Muslims, but do not seem to have been particularly religious. The family benefited tremendously from close connections with the Saudi royal family, which had closer ties with the West than many other Middle Eastern Muslim rulers of the time.

As far as can be determined, bin Laden's father died when he was about thirteen. The

different parts of the world, wherever Americans may be stationed. Thus, bin Laden is a threat to people across much of the globe.

Bin Laden poses a particular danger because of his ability to keep a very low profile. Ever since beginning his terrorist activities, bin Laden has been unusually elusive. His earliest efforts at building al-Qaeda were largely ignored by much of the rest of the world, and he has been careful to leave little direct evidence of his involvement in terrorist activities. He has consistently evaded detection and capture.

death entitled him to a significant share of his father's estate. This represented enough money to keep him comfortably wealthy throughout his life, although a large portion of the funds was—at least initially—kept in trust for him. Four years later, bin Laden married a Syrian woman. By 2001, he had four wives and at least sixteen children.

Bin Laden attended college in Jeddah, Saudi Arabia. At some point along the way, he joined a Saudi branch of the Muslim Brotherhood, the Islamic cultural and social service organization to which Hamas founder Ahmed Yassin also belonged. Being part of this group evidently helped bin Laden confirm his commitment to Islam. By the late 1970s, he had become much more openly religious than his parents had been.

At the time, bin Laden adopted a rather conservative interpretation of Islam, especially with regard to social issues. Although he had grown up in a relatively secular world with a heavy Western influence, he now began to distrust Western social standards. At college, he took several classes with conservative Muslim scholars. He seems to have adopted much of his early religious thought from these professors.

Before long, however, bin Laden's conservatism began to move into the realm of religious fanaticism. By 1979, his interpretation of Islam was in some ways out of step with the ideas of mainstream Muslims. Advocating a clean break from encroaching Western notions, he worked for a return to a more traditional Islamic government. He

A waterfront mosque stands tall in Jeddah, Saudi Arabia, the city where bin Laden went to college.

identified less and less with the Saudi state and secular Saudi culture. Instead, he began to see himself as a Muslim first and foremost, a vision that gave him a connection with Muslims across the world.

That same year, bin Laden left school and traveled to Afghanistan, a small, landlocked country in Central Asia. Bin Laden's decision was motivated by religion. Like Saudi Arabia, Afghanistan was a nation with an overwhelmingly Muslim population. However, it had been invaded by forces from the Soviet Union, an officially atheistic country. Bin Laden considered the attack on Afghanistan to be an attack on Islam itself, and he came to Afghanistan's defense.

Afghanistan

Bin Laden's experiences in Afghanistan were critical to his development as a terrorist. However, the role he played in helping the country's defenders—conservative Muslims known as the mujahideen—was probably not terrorist in itself. Nearly all of his activities were well within acceptable standards for a military operation. The mujahideen, after all, were fighting a war against the Soviet invaders. Bin Laden's early part in the conflict focused on destroying soldiers and military installations; as far as possible, he left innocent civilians alone.

Bin Laden made two important contributions to the war effort. One was monetary. He bought weapons, tanks, and other military equipment for the mujahideen, using the funds from his inheritance as well as proceeds from a family construction company in which he still held an interest. Using his family's construction equipment, he also built roads and tunnels for the mujahideen's use.

Bin Laden's other contribution was soldiers. Traveling across the Islamic world, he recruited thousands of Muslims whose ideas about Islam matched his. To help prepare them for the conflict, bin Laden built a training center that he called al-Qaeda—then only a complex of buildings and not yet an organization. He funded the center's costs primarily out of his own pocket, although he solicited funds from elsewhere in the Muslim world as well.

Of all his activities in Afghanistan, bin Laden's role in founding al-Qaeda is the only one that could be termed "terrorist." But even that claim is dubious. Most evidence suggests that al-Qaeda was, at least at first, simply a training center to help the mujahideen succeed in their war against the Soviet Union. In that sense, it was a base with a purpose similar to that of American military academies.

The conflict in Afghanistan dragged on for about ten years, ending in 1989 with the withdrawal of Soviet troops. The mujahideen had proved far more troublesome than the Soviet Union had predicted. Part of the reason was the help bin Laden gave to the Afghans. By one estimate, he spent some $3 billion of his own money to help defeat the Soviets, and the value of his al-Qaeda training center was incalculable.

The Soviet-Afghan War had several important effects on bin Laden's life and works. For one, the war reinforced his notion that his first loyalty was to his religion, rather than to any particular nation or state. In

A Soviet tank rolls out of Afghanistan and across the border to the Soviet Union.

Afghanistan, he had seen Muslims of many different nations working together to defend not only a nation but the entire Islamic world. Bin Laden's experiences in Afghanistan also taught him an important political lesson: Given sufficient resolve by the opposition, even a superpower could be defeated. That theme would loom large in bin Laden's later acts of terrorism.

Finally, there was al-Qaeda. Al-Qaeda had served an important purpose in training thousands of soldiers for Afghan defense. At the end of the war, however, bin Laden made no move to shut it down. Officially, it remained open as a training center for the Afghan army, a base for preparing and

recruiting soldiers should the Soviets return. Yet most experts now acknowledge that bin Laden had other plans in mind for the camp. Its resources could be used not merely to produce an Afghan army but also to train violent terrorists. Terrorist training at al-Qaeda may have already begun by the end of the war, but no Westerner knew it at the time.

The Gulf War

At the end of the Soviet-Afghan War, bin Laden returned to Saudi Arabia, where he became involved in another controversy. In late 1990, Iraq invaded its wealthy but tiny neighbor Kuwait. Kuwait called upon its ally, the United States, for help. The United States responded by fighting the Gulf War in Kuwait's defense. American military officials sent thousands of troops to the Middle East, including an estimated half-million soldiers posted to Saudi Arabia. The Saudi leaders were friendly toward the United States and hostile toward Iraq; they were happy to host these soldiers.

Bin Laden, in contrast, strongly disapproved of the American action. In his eyes, America had no business sending troops into the Islamic world at all. The fact that some American soldiers were stationed in Saudi Arabia particularly infuriated him. Because it is the site of some of the holiest places in Islam, Saudi Arabia holds a special place in the Muslim faith. "The American government has committed the greatest mistake in entering a peninsula [that is, Saudi Arabia] that no religion from among the non-Muslim nations has entered for 14 centuries," bin Laden complained. "Never has Islam suffered a greater disaster than this invasion."[45]

Bin Laden's disapproval of the American presence was also sparked by a growing hostility toward U.S. foreign policy. He was a staunch opponent of the Gulf War; he saw it as an American attempt to overrun a Muslim nation, just as the Soviets had done in Afghanistan. Israel was another sticking point. In the continuing conflict between Israel and its Arab neighbors, bin Laden charged, the United States always sided with Israel, thus supporting and encouraging Israeli violence. "Israeli troops are using American-made weapons," he pointed out. "The Americans made these weapons through the taxes collected from their citi-

U.S. soldiers survey their surroundings in Saudi Arabia during the Gulf War.

zens. So all of the American citizens . . . are part of the crime."[46]

The outcome of the Gulf War was not what bin Laden had hoped. Iraq was defeated and withdrew from Kuwait. In the aftermath of the war, the United States and its allies placed tight economic sanctions on Iraq, punishing it for being the aggressor. Bin Laden objected strenuously to the sanctions. By cutting off the shipment of valuable supplies, he asserted, the sanctions were killing thousands of Iraqi children. It was another reason for bin Laden to hate the United States.

Turning to Terror

Immediately following the Gulf War, however, bin Laden saved his angriest words for his own country. There had been long-standing conflict in Saudi Arabia between the relatively Westernized leaders of the government and the more conservative and traditional citizens of the country. Furious about the presence of the American troops, bin Laden now saw the Saudi government as a great evil. In his view, the nation's rulers were selling out Islam in a frantic desire to modernize.

During the next few months, bin Laden lost no opportunity to criticize the Saudi leaders and push for a return to a more traditionally Islamic state. The rulers were deeply offended by bin Laden's comments. In 1991, bin Laden relocated to Sudan, a more strictly Muslim country south of Egypt. It is not clear whether this decision was entirely bin Laden's or whether Saudi officials urged him to leave.

Officially, bin Laden came to Sudan to build roads, and in fact he did help improve the local transportation network considerably. But road building was not all that bin Laden accomplished. Since his move to Sudan, American authorities and intelligence sources in other countries have linked bin Laden to vio-

lent incidents in Africa, the Middle East, and elsewhere. Though his exact role in this terror is unclear, investigators say that they have strong evidence that he planned and funded these attacks. Bin Laden may have been involved in terrorist activity even before the end of the Soviet-Afghan War, but he had certainly begun sponsoring terrorist acts by 1992, soon after his arrival in Africa.

The first of these attacks occurred when U.S. soldiers took part in a peacekeeping mission in Somalia, a largely Muslim nation in eastern Africa. In 1992, terrorists placed bombs at two hotels used by American military personnel in Yemen, a nation across the Red Sea from Somalia. The attack killed no one. The following year, however, troops stationed in Somalia itself were not so lucky. Terrorists there shot down a U.S. helicopter

Somalis gather around a U.S. tank that is patrolling the streets of Mogadishu.

and carried out several other violent actions, including the murder of eighteen American soldiers in a late 1993 ambush.

However, bin Laden's earliest acts of terror were not confined to the Middle Eastern nations. In February 1993, terror came directly to the United States when a bomb exploded in a vehicle parked beneath the World Trade Center. Six people were killed and about a thousand more wounded in the blast. An investigation revealed that the bomb had been planted by a Pakistani named Ramzi Yousef. Arrested in New York, Yousef was sentenced to life in prison.

Blame

American intelligence experts doubted that Yousef had acted alone, and they did not believe that the terrorists responsible for the violence in Yemen and Somalia had independently planned and carried out their attacks. They began to search for a leader who might have ordered the terror from behind the scenes. Evidence soon surfaced suggesting that bin Laden might be the person they sought.

The suspicion certainly made sense. As a noted anti-American agitator, bin Laden had the desire to hurt U.S. citizens and to disrupt its military operations. Moreover, as a wealthy man with a strong following among conservative Muslims, bin Laden had the means and the support to carry out his plans. Finally, there were some clear connections between bin Laden and the men who actually carried out the attacks. Ramzi Yousef, for instance, lived for a while at a housing complex owned by bin Laden, and phone records

suggest that the two spoke on several occasions.

Actually pinning the attacks on bin Laden, however, proved much more difficult. Whereas some terrorist leaders brag about each successful operation, bin Laden has typically been much more circumspect. He denied knowing Yousef, and at the time he took no blame for the attacks in Yemen and Somalia. "I am a construction engineer and an agriculturalist,"[47] he told a reporter in response to the question of his involvement; he was not, he went on to add, a terrorist.

In the end, there was not enough evidence to prove that bin Laden had indeed ordered the attacks. American intelligence officials had to content themselves with watching him closely. That, however, was a difficult task. The strict Islamic government of Sudan had little liking for the United States and did not share intelligence information with American agents. Thus, accurate information about bin Laden's activities—even his whereabouts—was scarce. Some U.S. officials suspected that he was running at least three terrorist training camps in a remote part of Sudan, for example, but it was impossible to be sure.

Concerned about bin Laden's activities in Sudan, Saudi Arabia stripped him of his citizenship in 1994. If anything, the decision strengthened bin Laden's resolve. He was now more convinced than ever that the Saudi regime was hopelessly corrupt—and overly influenced by its U.S. allies. The loss of his citizenship did not stop the terror aimed at American targets. Instead, it increased the violence.

In 1995 and 1996, two bombs went off in Saudi Arabia, killing twenty-six—nearly all of them American soldiers—and injuring several hundred. Bin Laden once again disclaimed any responsibility for planning and ordering the attacks. But, as before, intelligence officials suspected that he was lying. Again, there were connections between bin Laden and the four Saudi men charged with the first of the bombings. Moreover, American and Saudi officials knew of no one else with both the power and the motivation to launch such attacks on Saudi territory. Once again, however, clear and unambiguous evidence linking bin Laden to the terror was lacking.

Jihad

For years, bin Laden had been outspoken in his anger at the West and at the Saudi government, but he had generally stopped short of seeming to encourage violence. In 1996, that changed when bin Laden declared a holy war, or jihad, against the U.S. government. This declaration called on Muslims to drive the Americans from the Muslim holy lands. "In our religion," bin Laden explained, "it is our duty to make jihad so that God's word is the one exalted to the heights and so that we drive the Americans away from all Muslim countries."[48]

The declaration of jihad did not lead to an immediate outbreak of violence against American troops. Many Muslims did not object to the presence of American troops, and many who did had no desire to use force against them. Even bin Laden's most devoted followers did not begin a killing spree. Nevertheless, the declaration wor-

In 1996 bin Laden, seen here in a still from a terrorist training video, declared a holy war against the United States.

ried American officials, who began to press the Sudanese government to exile bin Laden. Once away from his home base, American officials reasoned, bin Laden's influence would diminish.

Sudan soon bowed to the American pressure. Bin Laden, exiled for the second time, now headed for Afghanistan, where he had begun training soldiers to help the mujahideen almost twenty years earlier. The United States was pleased. Afghanistan was engaged in civil conflict at the time, and it was such a poor and undeveloped country that it seemed implausible that bin Laden could do much from such a base. Moreover, both Sudan and Saudi Arabia, acting on U.S. requests, had frozen bin

Laden's assets, which put much of his wealth out of his control.

But, once again, the decision backfired. The move to Afghanistan did not contain bin Laden. If anything, it made him even bolder—and brought him to a part of the world where it was even more difficult to monitor his activities and track his where-abouts than it had been in Sudan. Bin Laden quickly disappeared into the Afghan wilderness, but he had not given up the battle.

Ties with the Taliban

Before long, bin Laden was offering aid to the Taliban, a group of extremely conservative Muslims rapidly gaining the upper hand in Afghanistan's civil war. When the war came to an end, the Taliban controlled nearly all Afghan territory. With bin Laden's help, they instituted a repressive government based on fundamentalist Islamic principles, ideas so extreme that they were seen as dangerous even by most other Muslim countries.

With the help of the Taliban, in turn, bin Laden continued to build a terrorist network. He rededicated himself to al-Qaeda, expand-ing the base and bringing in men from across the Muslim world—perhaps twenty thou-sand by one estimate. Under its new rulers, Afghanistan was a compelling destination for deeply conservative Muslims eager to fight for their faith. Bin Laden was well placed to train them.

Even having been cut off from much of his wealth did not prove a problem. He set up other sources of funding for his terrorist activities, including founding organizations that solicited help from wealthy Muslims who shared his beliefs. Plus, the costs of the train-ing camps were not high. In today's world, explosives and weapons are not terribly expensive, and many budding terrorists paid "tuition" for their training.

More Acts of Terror

Since the Gulf War, bin Laden's hatred of the United States had steadily increased. In his eyes, the United States had committed a number of crimes against Islam: fighting and then sanctioning Iraq; stationing soldiers in Saudi territory; and supporting Israel. Now, with his exile from Sudan, he believed that the United States was on a mission to destroy him altogether. "Muslims burn with anger at America,"[49] he wrote in his statement of jihad. No doubt some did, but bin Laden burned more fiercely than most.

Safely in Afghanistan, bin Laden issued a fatwa, or religious ruling, in 1998. This doc-ument urged Muslims to kill all Americans, both civilians and military. Most of the world's Muslims called such an order con-tradictory to true Islamic teachings. But bin Laden stood firm. He did not accept criticism from Westerners who argued that it was immoral to target peaceful civilians as well as soldiers. In his view, Muslims were engaged in a war, and in a war, he explained, the rules were different.

It did not take long for his fatwa to have an effect. That August, bombs went off at the American embassies in the East African nations of Kenya and Tanzania. The blasts killed 301 people and injured thousands more. U.S. authorities soon arrested four men in conjunction with the attacks, all of them known to be members of al-Qaeda. All four were convicted and sentenced to life in prison without the possibility of parole.

As had been the case earlier in the 1990s, it proved impossible to directly link bin Laden with the crimes. The trial did, however, bring out some important information about the structure of al-Qaeda. Most of the testimony indicated that bin Laden was the group's ultimate leader, with responsibility for planning most of al-Qaeda's activities—although the bombers said that in this case they had acted independently.

The attack also indicated that bin Laden's power extended far beyond the borders of Afghanistan. During the trial of the four bombers, it became clear that al-Qaeda had become an international terrorist organization, with operatives in Africa, Asia, and elsewhere. Moreover, testimony showed that al-Qaeda had shared information, operatives, and strategies with several other terrorist organizations, including the militant Egyptian group Islamic Jihad and the Iranian organization known as Hezbollah.

Retaliation

After the embassy bombings, the United States did at last retaliate against bin Laden. Acting on orders from President Bill Clinton, the military used missiles to destroy suspected terrorist camps in Afghanistan and Sudan. However, Clinton's orders were unpopular.

Burned bodies lie beside the destruction caused by the 1998 explosion of the American embassy in Nairobi, Kenya.

Some suspected that he had ordered the attack simply to deflect attention from his own personal and political problems. Others were unsure whether bin Laden was actually behind the embassy bombings or worried that the attacks would be poorly received in other Muslim countries. This lack of support put a quick end to the missile strikes.

Bin Laden was not intimidated. In October 2000, terrorists killed seventeen American sailors aboard a ship docked in Yemen. As before, bin Laden denied responsibility for the action; still, he was widely suspected of having masterminded the scheme. But by this time, authorities believe, bin Laden was already hard at work planning an even bigger attack, an action that would strike directly at the heart of American commerce and government. It is a testimonial to the secrecy of al-Qaeda that Western intelligence experts had no idea of the group's plans.

September 11

On September 11, 2001, four planes took off from airports along the East Coast of the United States. Soon after takeoff, several hijackers commandeered each flight. They were armed not with guns but with knives, razors, and other sharp weapons. Their intention was to use the aircrafts as flying bombs.

On three of the flights, their plans succeeded. Shortly before nine in the morning, one of the airplanes struck one of the twin towers of the World Trade Center. Jet fuel burned out of control, trapping workers on the building's top floors. About fifteen minutes later, while officials still wondered if the crash had simply been a terrible accident, a second airliner crashed into the other tower.

Rescue workers from around New York City streamed into the towers to save as many people as they could. Unfortunately, many of those on the topmost floors of the center had no escape. The tragedy was compounded when the heat of the fire destroyed some of the towers' structural supports. Before long, both towers had crumbled to the ground, crushing nearly everyone still inside—including firefighters and police officers who had come to help.

The third plane, in the meantime, struck the Pentagon across the Potomac River from Washington, D.C. Here, damage was not as great as at the World Trade Center. Still, the destruction was significant. One side of the building was badly damaged. Many workers at the Pentagon were wounded, and a number of those in the immediate area of the crash were killed.

The fourth plane, in contrast, had been delayed taking off. So, the hijackers acted after the other planes had already hit their targets. When passengers contacted friends and family by cell phone, they learned that the first three planes had been used as suicide bombs. Understanding that they would probably die regardless, some of the passengers rushed the hijackers to try to take control of the plane. The terrorists' intended target will never be known; the aircraft crashed in rural Pennsylvania, killing all aboard.

"There Is America, Full of Fear"

In all, the hijackings caused the deaths of several thousand Americans. Suspicion quickly settled on bin Laden. Elusive and cautious as

The twin towers of the World Trade Center burn after hijacked airplanes crashed into them on September 11, 2001.

always, bin Laden neither denied nor confirmed complicity in the attacks. But again he left no doubt about his opinions on the disaster. "[America's] buildings were destroyed, thank God for that," he said on a videotape made soon after September 11. "There is America, full of fear. . . . Thank God for that."[50]

However, few experts doubted that bin Laden had been behind the attacks. His hatred of the United States made him a likely candidate. But just as telling was the power wielded by bin Laden. To plan and carry out an attack of this size required an enormous amount of support and personnel, and bin Laden had what it took. In particular, he had access to an international network of terror. "He's been singularly successful in unifying the diverse strands of terrorism," said an expert on the Middle East. "He's the first to be able to do it. It's money, charisma, being in the right place at the right time . . . [and] vision."[51]

U.S. president George W. Bush tried at first to use diplomatic channels to capture bin Laden. He urged the Taliban to hand him over peacefully, but the Taliban refused. In early October, the United States began firing missiles into Afghanistan. These missiles were aimed at military targets belonging to the Taliban and at al-Qaeda training sites.

Bin Laden had never had a high opinion of American military strength. "We have seen in the last decade . . . the weakness of the American soldier," [52] he told an interviewer shortly before the hijackings. Both he and Taliban leaders taunted the United States before the bombings began, saying that the American military would prove too afraid to fight a real war. They were wrong: U.S. weaponry, troops, and know-how proved to be more than a match for the limited resources of the Taliban.

In November, just a few weeks after the attacks began, Taliban resistance crumbled. U.S.-backed rebels from a group called the Northern Alliance swept through much of the country, displacing Taliban leaders. The official resistance was over, and some believed that bin Laden would soon give up or be captured. However, as the weeks went by, it became clear that that was not to be.

Endgame

As of December 2001, the search for bin Laden continued. Most American officials believed that he was holed up in a remote and well-guarded cave complex, complete with computers, satellite telephones, and heavy

A U.S. Navy sailor watches a helicopter take off as part of flight operations for Operation Enduring Freedom, the official name of U.S. efforts in Afghanistan.

weaponry. U.S. special forces combed the region, looking for possible hideouts. Officials put a $25 million bounty on bin Laden's head in hopes of convincing a friend to turn him in. At the same time, the U.S. military kept a close eye on Afghanistan's borders, suspecting that he might try to escape into Pakistan or another nearby country. Officials were determined to capture bin Laden and as many of his followers as they could.

Bin Laden and al-Qaeda have demonstrated their ability to execute devastating terrorist acts with ruthlessness and surprise. For nearly all Americans, the September 11 tragedy was completely unexpected. It seemed inconceivable that any organization could plan and carry out such a monstrous attack without some indication of what was to come. But it is clear that Americans had underestimated Osama bin Laden. His power was great, his hatred of the United States was intense, and his ability to keep a low profile was unsurpassed. The combination, in the end, was lethal.

Notes

Introduction: The Terrorists

1. Quoted in "Terrorist Groups Profiles." http://web.nps.navy.mil/~library/tgp/tgp main.htm.

Chapter One: Hamas

2. Quoted in Bob Hepburn, "Terror Campaign Proving Effective as Hamas Tries to Derail Peace," *Toronto Star*, October 23, 1994, p. E6+.
3. Quoted in Shaul Mishal and Avraham Sela, *The Palestinian Hamas*. New York: Columbia University Press, 2000, p. 63.
4. Quoted in "Sheikh Tried for Army Deaths," *Times* (London), January 4, 1990.
5. Quoted in Hepburn, "Terror Campaign Proving Effective as Hamas Tries to Derail Peace," p. E6+.
6. Quoted in Hepburn, "Terror Campaign Proving Effective as Hamas Tries to Derail Peace," p. E6+.
7. Quoted in Lee Hockstader, "Palestinians Find Heroes in Hamas," *Washington Post*, August 11, 2001, p. A1+.
8. Quoted in Laura Blumenfeld, "Blown Away," *Washington Post*, January 4, 1998, p. F1+.
9. Quoted in Hockstader, "Palestinians Find Heroes in Hamas," p. A1+.
10. Quoted in Marjorie Miller, "Among Palestinians, Freed Hamas Founder's Grasp Exceeds His Reach," *Los Angeles Times*, November 9, 1997, p. 8+.
11. Quoted in Mishal and Sela, *The Palestinian Hamas*, p. 52.
12. Quoted in Miller, "Among Palestinians, Freed Hamas Founder's Grasp Exceeds His Reach," p. 8+.

13. Quoted in Barbara Demick, "Spiritual Leader of Hamas Militant Group Decries Terror in Mideast," *St. Louis Post-Dispatch*, January 4, 1998, p. B7+.
14. Quoted in Blumenfeld, "Blown Away," p. F1+.

Chapter Two: Abimael Guzman and Shining Path

15. Quoted in Simon Strong, *Shining Path: Terror and Revolution in Peru*. New York: Times Books, 1992, p. 7.
16. Quoted in William R. Long, "Professor of Terror in Peru," *Los Angeles Times*, April 8, 1992, p. 1+.
17. Quoted in Philip Bennett, "A Blow to Shining Path: Guzman's Arrest Shatters an Image," *Boston Globe*, September 20, 1992, p. 73+.
18. Quoted in Long, "Professor of Terror in Peru," p. 1+.
19. Quoted in Strong, *Shining Path*, p. 26.
20. Quoted in Gabriella Gamini, "In the Killing Fields of Peru," *Manchester Guardian*, April 6, 1994.
21. Quoted in Gamini, "In the Killing Fields of Peru."
22. Quoted in Strong, *Shining Path*, p. 128.
23. Quoted in Long, "Professor of Terror in Peru," p. 1+.
24. Quoted in Monte Hayes, "Peru's Rebel Chief Gets Life Sentence," *New Orleans Times-Picayune*, October 8, 1992, p. A1+.
25. Quoted in Nathaniel C. Nash, "Shining Path 'Like a Wounded, Wild Animal' After Leader Seized," *Houston Chronicle*, November 29, 1992, p. 24+.

Chapter Three: The Irish Republican Army

26. Quoted in Peter Taylor, *Behind the Mask: The IRA and Sinn Fein.* New York: TV Books, 1997, p. 18.
27. Quoted in J. Bowyer Bell, *The Secret Army.* Cambridge, MA: MIT Press, 1979, p. 18.
28. Quoted in Terry Golway, *For the Cause of Liberty.* New York: Simon and Schuster, 2000, p. 268.
29. Quoted in Tim Pat Coogan, *The I.R.A.* New York: Praeger, 1970, p. 40.
30. Quoted in Golway, *For the Cause of Liberty,* p. 282.
31. Quoted in Taylor, *Behind the Mask,* p. 88.
32. Quoted in Taylor, *Behind the Mask,* p. 113.
33. Quoted in Jonathan Bartlett, ed., *Northern Ireland.* New York: H.W. Wilson, 1983, p. 100.
34. Quoted in Bartlett, *Northern Ireland,* p. 81.

Chapter Four: Timothy McVeigh

35. Quoted in David H. Hackworth and Peter Annin, "The Suspect Speaks Out," *Newsweek,* July 3, 1995, p. 23.
36. Quoted in Lou Michel and Dan Herbeck, *American Terrorist: Timothy McVeigh and the Oklahoma City Bombing.* New York: HarperCollins, 2001, p. 7.
37. Quoted in Richard A. Serrano, *One of Ours: Timothy McVeigh and the Oklahoma City Bombing.* New York: W.W. Norton, 1998, p. 21.
38. Quoted in Michel and Herbeck, *American Terrorist,* p. 76.
39. Quoted in Michel and Herbeck, *American Terrorist,* p. 120.
40. Quoted in Serrano, *One of Ours,* p. 78.
41. Quoted in "McVeigh Justifies Bombing," *Houston Chronicle,* May 29, 1998, p. 10+.
42. Quoted in Associated Press, "From a Cell in Colorado, McVeigh Talks," *Boston Globe,* August 18, 1997, p. A3+.
43. Quoted in Associated Press, "McVeigh Tells Newspaper He Expects That Courts Will Reject His Appeals," *St. Louis Post-Dispatch,* December 19, 1997, p. A15+.
44. Quoted in Associated Press, "In Final Hours, McVeigh Remains Defiant," *St. Louis Post-Dispatch,* June 11, 2001, p. A11.

Chapter Five: Osama bin Laden and al-Qaeda

45. Quoted in Robin Wright, "Saudi Dissident a Prime Suspect in Blasts, Terror," *Los Angeles Times,* August 14, 1998, p. A1+.
46. Quoted in Michael Cabbage, "Biography of a Terrorist," *Denver Post,* October 15, 2001, p. A10+.
47. Quoted in Robert Fisk, "Anti-Soviet Warrior Puts His Army on the Road to Peace," *Independent,* December 6, 1993, p. 10+.
48. Quoted in "Osama bin Laden v. the U.S.: Edicts and Statements." www.pbs.org/wgbh/pages/frontline/shows/binladen/who/edicts.html.
49. Quoted in "Osama bin Laden v. the U.S."
50. Associated Press, "From in Hiding, a Message of Hate," *Poughkeepsie Journal,* October 8, 2001, p. 9A+.
51. Quoted in Paul Watson, Tyler Marshall, and Bob Drogin, "Osama bin Laden," *Pittsburgh Post-Gazette,* September 16, 2001, p. A4+.
52. Quoted in Laura K. Egendorf, ed., *Terrorism: Opposing Viewpoints.* San Diego: Greenhaven Press, 2000, p. 125.

For Further Reading

Christopher Dobson and Ronald Payne, *The Terrorists.* Rev. ed. New York: Facts On File, 1990. A good basic source of information on terrorism; describes some important terrorist leaders and groups.

Laura K. Egendorf, ed., *Terrorism: Opposing Viewpoints.* San Diego: Greenhaven Press, 2000. A compilation of articles and perspectives on terrorism throughout the world.

Michael Kronenwetter, *Northern Ireland.* New York: Franklin Watts, 1990. A strong overview of the issues in Ulster; even-handed and thorough. Includes some information on the IRA.

Thomas Raynor, *Terrorism: Past, Present, Future.* New York: Franklin Watts, 1982. Dated but nevertheless an interesting and thorough look at terrorism around the world.

Works Consulted

Books

Jonathan Bartlett, ed., *Northern Ireland.* New York: H.W. Wilson, 1983. Useful information about the IRA in the context of the history of Northern Ireland.

J. Bowyer Bell, *The Secret Army.* Cambridge, MA: MIT Press, 1979. The story of the IRA through 1979; detailed and thorough.

Tim Pat Coogan, *The I.R.A.* New York: Praeger, 1970. The history of the IRA, with emphasis on its early years.

Terry Golway, *For the Cause of Liberty.* New York: Simon and Schuster, 2000. An informative look at the history of Irish resistance to British rule. Includes information on the IRA, both in the past and in more recent times.

Lou Michel and Dan Herbeck, *American Terrorist: Timothy McVeigh and the Oklahoma City Bombing.* New York: HarperCollins, 2001. A thorough and interesting account of McVeigh's life and activities, based in part on interviews McVeigh gave the authors while he was imprisoned.

Shaul Mishal and Avraham Sela, *The Palestinian Hamas.* New York: Columbia University Press, 2000. A scholarly study of the founding, structure, and activities of Hamas.

Richard A. Serrano, *One of Ours: Timothy McVeigh and the Oklahoma City Bombing.* New York: W.W. Norton, 1998. A careful look at the Oklahoma City bombing.

Claire Sterling, *The Terror Network.* New York: Holt, Rinehart, and Winston, 1981. Discusses the connections between various terrorist organizations, along with descriptions of some of the groups' activities and origins.

Simon Strong, *Shining Path: Terror and Revolution in Peru.* New York: Times Books, 1992. Describes Shining Path's rise to power and later activities, concluding with Guzman's arrest. The author is a journalist who lived for several years in Lima, Peru.

Peter Taylor, *Behind the Mask: The IRA and Sinn Fein.* New York: TV Books, 1997. Well-written and well-documented look at the connections between the IRA and the political party Sinn Fein.

Periodicals

Associated Press, "From a Cell in Colorado, McVeigh Talks," *Boston Globe,* August 18, 1997.

———, "From in Hiding, a Message of Hate," *Poughkeepsie Journal,* October 8, 2001.

———, "In Final Hours, McVeigh Remains Defiant," *St. Louis Post-Dispatch,* June 11, 2001.

———, "McVeigh Tells Newspaper He Expects That Courts Will Reject His Appeals," *St. Louis Post-Dispatch,* December 19, 1997.

Philip Bennett, "A Blow to Shining Path: Guzman's Arrest Shatters an Image," *Boston Globe,* September 20, 1992.

Laura Blumenfeld, "Blown Away," *Washington Post,* January 4, 1998.

James Brooke, "How Police Pulled Off Peru's 'Arrest of the Century,'" *San Francisco Chronicle,* September 15, 1992.

Michael Cabbage, "Biography of a Terrorist," *Denver Post*, October 15, 2001.

George J. Church, "The Matter of Tim McVeigh," *Time*, August 14, 1995.

John Cloud, "What Is Al-Qaeda Without Its Boss?" *Time*, November 26, 2001.

Malcolm Coad, "Peru on Brink of Peace After Guerrilla Chief's U-Turn," *Manchester Guardian*, October 18, 1993.

Barbara Demick, "Spiritual Leader of Hamas Militant Group Decries Terror in Mideast," *St. Louis Post-Dispatch*, January 4, 1998.

Robert Fisk, "Anti-Soviet Warrior Puts His Army on the Road to Peace," *Independent*, December 6, 1993.

Glenn Frankel, "What Does Hamas Want?" *Cleveland Plain Dealer*, October 28, 1994.

Gabriella Gamini, "In the Killing Fields of Peru," *Manchester Guardian*, April 6, 1994.

David H. Hackworth and Peter Annin, "The Suspect Speaks Out," *Newsweek*, July 3, 1995.

Monte Hayes, "Peru's Rebel Chief Gets Life Sentence," *New Orleans Times-Picayune*, October 8, 1992.

Bob Hepburn, "Terror Campaign Proving Effective as Hamas Tries to Derail Peace," *Toronto Star*, October 23, 1994.

Lee Hockstader, "Israeli Missiles Kill Hamas Leader," *Chicago Tribune*, November 24, 2001.

———, "Palestinians Find Heroes in Hamas," *Washington Post*, August 11, 2001.

"Israel Seizes Dozens in Effort to Curb a Moslem Movement," *New York Times*, October 21, 1988.

"Israelis Kill 2 Palestinian Leaders," *Houston Chronicle*, August 1, 2001.

Brad Knickerbocker, "A McVeigh Legacy: Militias Wane," *Christian Science Monitor*, June 11, 2001.

Michael Kranish and Indira A.R. Lakshmanan, "Fighting Terror: The Trail," *Boston Globe*, October 28, 2001.

William R. Long, "Professor of Terror in Peru," *Los Angeles Times*, April 8, 1992.

Eric Lyman, "Shining Path Guerrillas Weaker, but Still Considered Threat to Peru," *Houston Chronicle*, September 12, 1997.

"McVeigh Justifies Bombing," *Houston Chronicle*, May 29, 1998.

Marjorie Miller, "Among Palestinians, Freed Hamas Founder's Grasp Exceeds His Reach," *Los Angeles Times*, November 9, 1997.

William D. Montalbano, "Alive or Dead? Guzman—Messiah of Peru Terror," *Los Angeles Times*, October 6, 1986.

Nathaniel C. Nash, "Guzman's Arrest Ends 12-Year Mystery," *Houston Chronicle*, September 15, 1992.

———, "Shining Path 'Like a Wounded, Wild Animal' After Leader Seized," *Houston Chronicle*, November 29, 1992.

Romesh Ratnesar, "The Hunt for bin Laden," *Time*, November 26, 2001.

Bruce Shapiro, "McVeigh: Done to Death," *Nation*, July 2, 2001.

"Sheikh Tried for Army Deaths," *Times* (London), January 4, 1990.

Kevin Toolis, "The Last Republicans," *Manchester Guardian*, June 13, 1998.

Paul Watson, Tyler Marshall, and Bob Drogin, "Osama bin Laden," *Pittsburgh Post-Gazette*, September 16, 2001.

Robin Wright, "Saudi Dissident a Prime Suspect in Blasts, Terror," *Los Angeles Times,* August 14, 1998.

Internet Sources
"Osama bin Laden: Biography." www.pbs.org/wgbh/pages/frontline/shows/binladen/who/bio2.html.

"Osama bin Laden v. the U.S.: Edicts and Statements." www.pbs.org/wgbh/pages/frontline/shows/binladen/who/edicts.html.

"Terrorist Groups Profiles." http://web.nps.navy.mil/~library/tgp/tgpmain.htm.

World Islamic Front, "Jihad Against Jews and Crusaders." www.fas.org/irp/world/para/docs/980223-fatwa.htm.

Index

shifting alliances in, 49
signs peace treaty with England, 47
Irish Citizens' Army, 45
Irish Parliament, 46, 47
Irish Republican Army (IRA)
  bombs used by, 53, 54
  Catholic policing by, 52
  changes in, 54–55
  creation of, 46
  faction groups of, 55
  forms constitution, 48
  goal of, in 1922, 48
  leaders of, loss of, 49
  members of, imprisonment of, 53–54
  mission of, 42, 54
  origins of, 42
  political activities of, 42, 46
  popular support for, 46, 47, 48, 51
  raids on British soldiers, 47
  reaction to peace treaty, 47–48
  recent activities of, 54
  roots of, 43–46
  signs cease-fire agreement, 55
  strategy shift in, 49
  tactics used by, 51–52
  terrorist acts, 46, 47–48, 52, 53
  weapons bought for, 51
  weapons used by, 53, 54
Irish Republican Brotherhood, 45, 46
Irish Volunteers, 46
Islam, founding of, 12
Islamic Jihad, 79
Islamic principles, 15
Islamic Resistance Movement, 15
  see also Hamas
Israel
  bans resistance groups, 16
  formation of government in, 13
  history of, 11–12
  holy war against, 15–16
  police violence in, 20
  territorial expansion of, 13

James I (king of England), 44
James II (king of England), 44
Japanese suicide bombers, 19

Jews
  in ancient times, 12
  flee from Muslim rule, 12
  reclaim land in Israel, 12–13
  Zionist, 12–13
jihad (holy war), 15, 77
Jones, Stephen, 66

Kenya, bombings in, 78–79
Koran, 15
Kuwait, 73–74

La Torre, Augusta, 32, 38
"left-wing," 10
liberals, definition of, 10
Libya, weapons from, 51
Londonderry (Ulster), 49
London Stock Exchange, 53
Lynch, Liam, 47, 49

MacStiofain, Sean, 51
MacSwiney, Terence, 47, 54
Mao Tse-tung, 30–31, 34
Mariategui, Jose Carlos, 31
Marx, Karl, 28
Marxism, 28, 29
McGuinness, Martin, 55
McKee, Billy, 51
McKevitt, Mickey, 54
McVeigh, Bill, 58
McVeigh, Mickey, 58
McVeigh, Timothy
  antigovernment views of, 61–63
  appeals guilty verdict, 67
  arrest of, 66
  carries out Oklahoma bombing, 64–65
  childhood, 58
  emotional instability of, 61
  fails special forces exam, 60–61
  family dynamics of, 58
  fights in Gulf War, 60
  interest in survivalism, 58–59
  joins army, 59
  leaves army, 61
  lethal injection death of, 68
  morality of, 10, 64

Picture Credits

About the Author

Stephen Currie is the author of more than forty books and many magazine articles. Among his nonfiction titles are *Polar Explorers, Issues in Immigration,* and *Life in the Trenches,* all for Lucent Books, and *We Have Marched Together: The Working Children's Crusade.* He grew up in Chicago and now lives in Poughkeepsie, New York, with his wife, Amity, and two children, Irene and Nicholas.